New Horizons in Workplace Well-Being

Satinder Dhiman
Editor

New Horizons in Workplace Well-Being

Reimagining Human Flourishing

Editor
Satinder Dhiman
School of Business
Woodbury University
Burbank, CA, USA

ISBN 978-3-031-17240-3   ISBN 978-3-031-17241-0   (eBook)
https://doi.org/10.1007/978-3-031-17241-0

This Palgrave Macmillan imprint is published by the registered company Springer Nature
Switzerland AG
The registered company address is: Gewerbestrasse 11, 6330 Cham, Switzerland

This volume is dedicated to
all seekers and practitioners of Workplace well-being,
who are committed to living a life of meaning,
for the common good!

INTRODUCTION

*Our days are so empty, filled with activities of every kind—business, specu-
lation, meditation, sorrow and joy. In spite of all this, our lives are empty.
Strip someone of position, power or money, and what are they? One had all
that show outwardly but is empty and shallow inwardly. One cannot have
both inner and outer riches. The inner fullness far outweighs the outer. One
can be robbed of the outer; outer events shattering what has been carefully
built up. But inner riches are incorruptible, nothing can touch them, for
they have not been put together by the mind. ~J. Krishnamurti*[1]

This book presents strategies and tools to cultivate human flourishing
in the present-day boundary-less work environment. Anchored in the
moral and spiritual dimension of well-being, it draws upon several allied
fields such as workplace wellness in business and psychology. It utilizes
findings from positive psychology, social psychology, quantum physics,
organizational behavior, and the world's contemplative wisdom traditions to support the case for workplace flourishing. Research shows that
organizations with higher levels of employee engagement routinely out-
perform those with lower employee engagement. This book provides
valuable insights into why employee well-being is such a powerful driver
of employee performance and engagement and what organizations can do
to enhance workplace flourishing and fulfillment.

---

[1] Krishnamurti, J. (2020). *Happy Is the One Who Is Nothing: Letters to a young Friend.*
Watkins., p. 25.

Chapters cover such themes as analyzing the causes of workplace disengagement and pathways to employee engagement; self-transformation as a prelude to transform organizations; mindfulness as framework to enhance human flourishing; and understanding the phenomenon of empowerment and strategies to foster it.

We present below a synoptic overview of the chapters in this volume:

- In chapter one, Satinder Dhiman draws upon the key lessons of Stoic philosophy to achieve workplace well-being and human flourishing. Humanity is passing through one of its toughest and uncertain times in recent memory. A tiny virus has shaken the whole edifice of human endeavors, underscored the fleeting nature of human structures, and has highlighted the precariousness of our organizations and institutions. The COVID-19 pandemic has also reignited the need for spiritual and moral transformation, both at the personal and professional levels. It has also heightened the need and concern for human and organizational well-being and flourishing. This chapter concludes with the perspective that we all need to work humbly together with each other, albeit with Stoic equanimity and calm, to combat the after-effects of the pandemic and stay constructive and strong-willed. Only then we can hope for a shared, sustainable future for humanity.

- In chapter two, Satish Modh draws upon the timeless wisdom of Srimad Bhagavad Gita, the Indian spiritual text *par excellence*, to present a perspective of self-transformation as the prelude to organizational transformation. As the Gita says, one has to make an effort to constantly transform oneself in life without degrading oneself. If one can do this, it can help the self, the organization, and the work environment. This chapter aims to provide a road map for self-transformation which can lead to transforming the organization. An effective organizational transformation cannot happen without self-transformation of those who are involved in leading the change. The self-transformation includes focusing on one's value system, strengthening one's resolve, dealing with people in the organization and finally the work itself.

- In chapter three, Laura E. Garza-Meza, Luis Portales, and Nancy E. Westrup-Villarrea present a study of mindfulness in Mexican organizations as an effective way to increase individual and organizational well-being. It presents the benefits perceived on a personal and organizational level by employees of two different organizations that have mindfulness programs. The creation of these programs within their respective organizations took different paths; while in one organization the impulse and creation came from top management, in the other, middle managements created the mindfulness programs. The study followed a qualitative approach, with the interest of recovering the voice of the participants and knowing these benefits in greater depth. In the first section, the authors present a brief review of mindfulness construct and its origins. It briefly presents the Mexican context in which the interviews were conducted, as well as the characteristics of the interviewees. The third section presents the results of mindfulness on a personal level, how the collaborators see it and how they apply it in their day-to-day lives. The fourth section presents the results at the organizational level, according to several dimensions.
- In chapter four, Varinder Kumar discusses different themes and obstacles in meaning in life after undertaking phenomenological study of different leaders from different fields. The study finds different themes of meaning in life like *ananda* or bliss, happiness and peace of mind, sense of direction, and responsibility for others' well-being. The obstacles to meaning in life include greed, selfish behavior, worldly passions, and confinement to lower order needs. The leaders should overcome these obstacles and realize meaning in life for their spiritual unfolding as well as for the betterment of the organization.
- In chapter five, Nidhi Kaushal notes that the traditional wisdom contained in Indian folklore has always been full of its teachings, policies, and morals, which reflects its implications in the field of organizational development through the perspective of psychological wellness and prosperity. It has a zenith elegance of personality enrichment through the aspect of values and humanity and is helpful

in equipping the organizational people with the qualities of self-leadership through self-transformation, perspective shifts, a new visionary approach, group morale, and the skill of managing the change. This chapter highlights the significance of ethnical as well as contemplative wisdom and its efficacy and cogency in identifying the strategies and measures for the leaders in the modern organizational system.

Live rationally, well.

Satinder Dhiman

CONTENTS

1 Attaining Workplace Well-Being and Human
  Flourishing: The Stoic Way   1
  Satinder Dhiman

2 Self-Transformation as a Prelude to Transform
  Organizations Based on the Ancient Traditions   15
  Satish Modh

3 Mindfulness in Mexican Organizations: An Effective
  Way to Increase Individual and Organizational
  Well-Being   35
  Laura E. Garza-Meza, Luis Portales,
  and Nancy E. Westrup-Villarreal

4 Pursuit of Meaning in Life and Human Flourishing:
  A Phenomenological Study   57
  Varinder Kumar

5 The Reference to Contemplative Indian Traditional
  Wisdom of Flourishing and Fulfillment Regarding
  the Organizational Workplace   77
  Nidhi Kaushal

Index   107

Contents

NOTES ON CONTRIBUTORS

Satinder Dhiman, Editor

Professor of Management at Woodbury University, Burbank, California, Dr. Dhiman serves as the Associate Dean, Chair, and Director of the M.B.A. Program. With an interdisciplinary research agenda encompassing *organization behavior, workplace spirituality, workplace well-being and fulfillment, sustainability, servant leadership, mindfulness, social entrepreneurship, education, organization development, and Eastern and Western philosophy in leadership*, Professor Dhiman holds a Ph.D. in Social Sciences from Tilburg University, Netherlands, an Ed.D. in Organizational Leadership from Pepperdine University, Los Angeles, an M.B.A. from West Coast University, Los Angeles, and a Master's degree in

Commerce from Panjab University, Chandigarh, India, having earned the Gold Medal. *He has also completed advanced Executive Leadership Programs at Harvard, Stanford, and Wharton.*

His academic leadership experience includes having served as the Chair for a special M.B.A. Program for the Mercedes-Benz executives, China, as a Distinguished Visiting Professor at the Tecnológico de Monterrey, Guadalajara campus, Mexico; as E-Commerce curriculum lead advisor, Universidad Francisco Gavidia, El Salvador, coordinator for the M.B.A. Student Los Angeles Fieldtrip Program for Berlin University for Professional Studies (DUW), accreditation mentor to Sustainability Management School (SUMAS), Gland, Switzerland. During Dec. 12–15, 2019, he was invited by Monash University, Australia, to lead a track in Spirituality in Management at the 16th International Conference in Business Management. He has served as the President (2016–2018), (2022–present), and as a distinguished *Patron* (2019-2021) for the International Chamber for Service Industry (ICSI).

Recognized as a strategic thinker for his pioneering contributions to the field of transformational leadership, workplace spirituality, workplace well-being, sustainability, and fulfillment in personal and professional arena, Professor Dhiman is a sought after Keynote speaker at regional, national, and international conferences such as the prestigious TEDx Conference @ College of the Canyons in Santa Clarita, California. Since then, he has led several major national and international conferences as co-organizer and/or as track chair.

Recipient of several national and international academic and professional honors and awards in teaching, scholarship, and service, Professor Dhiman was awarded the Woodbury University Ambassador of the Year Award in 2015 and 2017 and M.B.A. Professor of the Year Award in 2015; Scholarly and Creative Writing Award, 2019; Most Valuable M.B.A. Professor Award, 2018; Most Inspirational and Most Charismatic M.B.A. Teacher Award 2012, 2013/2014/2018; the Steve Allen Excellence in Education Award in 2006, and the prestigious *ACBSP International Teacher of the Year Award in 2004.* Most recently, he chaired a symposium at the Academy of Management that received the "2019 Best Symposium Proposal and Showcase Symposium" Award by the MSR Division.

Professor Dhiman's scholarly accomplishments include over 65 professional conference presentations, over 150 invitations to be a keynote speaker, over 100 online webinars, participation in plenary sessions, conference track chair sessions, leading symposiums and webinars, and scores of distinguished guest lectures and creative workshops—*nationally and internationally.* He has published over 70 peer-reviewed journal articles and book chapters. As author, translator, editor, co-author, co-editor of over 40 management, leadership, spirituality, sustainability, and accounting-related books and research monographs, his most recent books include Leadership after COVID-19: Working Together toward a Sustainable Future (2022—Springer, with Marques). New Horizons in Management, Leadership and Sustainability (2021—Springer, with Samaratunge); Bhagavad Gītā and Leadership: A Catalyst for Organizational Transformation (2019—Palgrave Macmillan); Managing by the Bhagavad Gītā: Timeless Lessons for Today's Managers (2018—Springer; with Amar); *Holistic Leadership* (Palgrave 2017), *Gandhi and Leadership* (Palgrave 2015), *Seven Habits of Highly Fulfilled People* (2012); and co-editing and co-authoring, with Marques, *Spirituality and Sustainability* (Springer 2016), *Leadership Today* (Springer, 2016), *Engaged Leadership* (Springer, 2018), New Horizons in Positive Leadership and Change (Springer, 2020), and Social Entrepreneurship and Corporate Social Responsibility (Springer, 2020).

He has also translated several Indian spiritual classics into English, including the *Sahaja Gītā.*

He is the *Editor-in-Chief* of *seven* multi-author *M*ajor Reference *W*orks: *Springer Handbook of Engaged Sustainability* (2018—Springer International, Switzerland) and *Palgrave Handbook of Workplace Spirituality and Fulfillment* (2018—Palgrave Macmillan, USA); Routledge Companion to Mindfulness at Work (2020); Palgrave Handbook of Workplace Wellbeing—A (2021—Palgrave Macmillan); *Routledge Companion to Leadership and Change* (2022—Routledge, UK); *The Palgrave Handbook of Servant Leadership* (2022—Palgrave Macmillan, USA; with Roberts); *The Springer Handbook of Global Leadership and Followership* (2022—Springer International, Switzerland; with Marques, Schmieder-Ramirez, and Malakyan).

Additionally, he serves as the *Editor-in-Chief* of *Palgrave Studies in Workplace Spirituality and Fulfillment;* Routledge Frontiers in Sustainable Business ; *the General Editor of a series entitled Routledge Frontiers in Sustainable Business Practice (the Series);* and lead editor of *Springer Series in Management, Change, Strategy and Positive Leadership.*

Some of his forthcoming titles include Leading without Power : A Model of Highly Fulfilled Leaders (2022—Palgrave Macmillan); *Conscious Consumption: Healthy, Humane and Sustainable Living* (2022—Routledge, UK); *Wise Leadership for Turbulent Times* (2022—Routledge, UK); and *Creative Leadershift: Discover. Innovate. Enact.* (2022—Routledge, with Chandra Handa). He has published research with his colleagues in *Journal of Values-Based Leadership, Organization Development Journal, Journal of Management Development, Journal of Social Change, Journal of Applied Business and Economics*, and *Performance Improvement*.

Professor Dhiman has served as Accreditation Consultant, Evaluator, and Site Visit Team Leader for the Accreditation Council for Business Schools and Programs (ACBSP) for more than 25 universities in America, Canada, Europe, and Asia. He is the Founder-Director of Forever Fulfilled, a Los Angeles-based Well-being Consultancy that focuses on workplace wellness, workplace spirituality, and self-leadership.

Laura E. Garza-Meza, Ed.D. Associate Professor within Universidad de Monterrey's business school teaching Organization Development and Change. She graduated from Pepperdine's doctoral program on organization change. She has continued certifications in the following fields: Ontological coach by the International Coach Federation; Mindfulness Coach by Koru; and Lego Serious Play ty the Association of Master Trainers by Lego. Additionally, she has been a consultant in change interventions in public and private organizations. Her purpose has been to facilitate the awakeness of consciousness by forming sustainable communities to contribute a more human society.

Nidhi Kaushal holds a Ph.D. in Management Studies from the Indian Institute of Technology, Roorkee. She holds a Master's degree in Business Administration and a Bachelor's degree in Computer Science from Kurukshetra University, India as well. She has been interested and indulged in research work related to Entrepreneurship, Leadership, Wisdom Literature, Management, and Indigenous Studies. During her PhD, she has identified the indigenous studies of literature and folklore related to Leadership and Management and presented her work at various international conferences and research publications across the globe. Working as a researcher, she is exploring Leadership with the study of Creative writings and ancient Indian scriptures, and this is her contribution to the academic research.

Varinder Kumar formerly a chairperson and an Associate Professor, N.J.S.A. Government College, Kapurthala (Punjab, India), currently serves as a Principal, Government College of Education, Jalandhar (Punjab, India). He holds an MCom from Panjab University Chandigarh (having earned the Gold Medal) and is currently working on his PhD in workplace spirituality. He has authored more than 30 books on Business Communication, Soft Skills, Human Values, and Professional Ethics which are prescribed in syllabuses of different Indian Universities. His areas of interest include spirituality at workplace, transformational leadership, and creativity.

Satish Modh, Ph.D. has more than 10 years of experience as a Professor in the Indian university system and more than 25 years of experience in the Indian aviation Industry. He is particularly well known for his research on Indian value systems and its application to ethical management. He was invited to speak on ethics and Bhagavad Gita at various universities in the USA including University of Southern California, University of North Carolina, San Diego State University, University of Central Florida, Athens State University, University of Washington (Seattle Campus), UT Dallas, UT Austin, Ohio State University and Michigan State University. Prof Modh was given 'Outstanding Reviewer Award' at Academy of Management Conference, Boston 2019 (MSR Interest Group).

Luis Portales has a Ph.D. in Social Sciences and a Master's in Digital Transformation and Business Development. He is a research professor at the University of Monterrey (UDEM), where he directed the Center for Well-being Studies and co-found the Social Transformation Lab. Since 2013 he has been a member of the National System of Researchers, Level I, and has published more than 30 indexed articles and 5 books. He has carried out several social impact assessments for municipal governments, NGOs, and companies. He is a consultant on ethics, social responsibility, sustainability, social business models for organizations, and impact assessments

Nancy E. Westrup-Villarreal, Ed.D. Since the year 2000 Nancy has worked for Universidad de Monterrey (UDEM) teaching Organization Development and Change within its business division. Previously, she worked for an international consulting firm TAI facilitating the implementation of Total Quality Systems in organizations located in Mexico, Costa Rica, Colombia, Venezuela, and Chile, as well as throughout the

USA and Canada. As a UDEM Emeritus Professor, she facilitated working with MDOC students in other cities such as Prague, Stockholm, and Beijing. Currently, she is a "shadow consultant" for UDEM students' final projects. For these reasons, she is a legal citizen of Mexico and the USA, but also enjoys declaring herself a citizen of the world.

LIST OF TABLES

Table 2.1   The seven energies, their attributes, and influences   26
Table 3.1   Classification of interviewees by company, years
            of practice, and time dedicated to the practice
            of mindfulness   42

CHAPTER 1

Attaining Workplace Well-Being and Human Flourishing: The Stoic Way

Satinder Dhiman

Abstract This chapter draws upon the key lessons of Stoic philosophy to achieve workplace well-being and human flourishing. Humanity is passing through one of its toughest and uncertain times in recent memory. A tiny virus has shaken the whole edifice of human endeavors, underscored the fleeting nature of human structures, and has highlighted the precariousness of our organizations and institutions. The COVID-19 pandemic has also reignited the need for spiritual and moral transformation, both at the personal and professional levels. It has also heightened the need and concern for human and organizational well-being and flourishing. This chapter concludes with the perspective that we all need to work humbly together with each other, albeit with Stoic equanimity and calm, to combat the after-effects of the pandemic and stay constructive and strong-willed. Only then we can hope for a shared, sustainable future for humanity.

S. Dhiman (✉)
School of Business, Woodbury University, Burbank, CA, USA
e-mail: Satinder.Dhiman@woodbury.edu

Keywords Workplace well-being · Human flourishing · Eudaimonia · Covid-19 pandemic · Stoicism · Marcus Aurelius · Epictetus · Seneca

INTRODUCTION

Humanity is passing through one of its toughest and uncertain times, indeed; perhaps the toughest it has ever experienced before in recent memory. A tiny virus has shaken the whole edifice of human endeavors and has left humanity gasping for breath. It has been a humbling realization that we are not in charge of the show! It has underscored the fleeting nature of human preoccupations and structures and has highlighted the precariousness of our organizations and institutions. Perhaps the deep disruption of the COVID-19 pandemic is just one expression of a wider pattern of systemic disruptions and challenges that organizations and its leaders will be facing over the next decade.

The COVID-19 pandemic has affected all of us and raised many questions about the ways we work, live our lives, and lead our organizations. During such turbulent times, the older wisdom traditions such as Stoicism can be helpful. Now that the impending danger of the COVID-19 pandemic is slowly giving way to a protracted state of caution and restraint, we can benefit from taking a Stoic perspective in dealing with its slings and arrows.

The COVID-19 pandemic has also reignited the need for spiritual and moral transformation, both at the personal and professional levels. No society or country can endure without a spiritual basis, a moral basis, a recognition of the value of fellowship, our sisterhood, brotherhood, and neighborhood. Such a sublime conception of the higher life ends all troubles, frictions, hatreds, and discords automatically. It has become abundantly clear that we all need to work humbly together with each other, albeit with Stoic equanimity and calm, to combat the after-effects of the pandemic and stay constructive and strong-willed. Only then we can hope for a shared, sustainable future for humanity.

Need for and Importance of Workplace Well-Being and Human Flourishing

The current context has also heightened the need and concern for human and organizational well-being and flourishing. There is a greater realization to live a life that is *eudaimôn*, the term the ancient Greek philosophers used for a life "well-lived" marked by "happiness," "fulfillment" or "flourishing." It is a sobering realization that personal flourishing or well-being (*eudaimonia*) or living well (*eu zén*) is the foundation upon which the edifice of workplace well-being can be built securely; for, organizational well-being is the aggregate of the well-being of its constituent individuals and *politics is ethics writ large*. If one needs to *be* the change one wants to bring about in the world, as Gandhi has averred, then the road to workplace happiness begins with first cultivating virtuous happiness at the individual level.

Eudaimonia: The Supreme Concern of All the Sages!

All classical systems of thought—secular and sacred alike—are in agreement that the supreme good of human life is *eudaimonia* and that living a life of moral virtue is the path to abiding happiness. *Eudaimonia* (generally translated as "happiness," "flourishing," or "living well" or "well-being") is also a key concept in all ethical and political philosophy. The Greek wisdom tradition equates well-being with living a virtuous life; that is, a life lived in accordance with four cardinal virtues—wisdom, justice, moderation, and courage. It garners the view that moral virtue is the gateway to happiness and that *being good* and *being happy* are vitally *interlinked*. The *eudaimonic* happiness is not a passing mood or a fleeting feeling of elation but rather an abiding state of felicity emanating from leading a life that is worth living—a life of virtue or moral excellence.

The wisdom of virtuous living is particularly relevant in the present turbulent times when humanity seems to have lost its moral and spiritual bearings. If "an unexamined life is not worth living," as Socrates averred in *Apology* (38a), then self-examination—the "regular monitoring and assessment of our own moral progress"—becomes the whetstone on which to hone one's character and gauge one's success in attaining happiness and well-being. *Being* good and *doing* good then becomes synonymous with living a happy, flourishing life. Plato sums up the essence of virtuous life and leadership in this final recommendation: "Always follow the upward path of righteousness, practicing justice with the help of wisdom" (*Republic* 621c).

Beware of Barrenness of a Busy Life!

Life is a strange business. Happy is the one who is nothing.
—Krishnamurti[1]

One is wonderstruck with the profundity of Krishnamurti's insight. He doesn't say, happy is the man who *has* nothing. He is pointing out that happy is the man who *is* nothing. Human flourishing has nothing to do with what one *has* or *does not have*. It has everything to do with what one thinks one *is*. We need to marvel at the beauty of the distinction between *having* and *being*. Krishnamurti's main concern is true freedom: freedom from all authority of not just others but of one's own ego as well.

Elsewhere commenting on the barrenness of a busy life, Krishnamurti (2020, p. 25) laments:

> Our days are so empty, filled with activities of every kind—business, speculation, meditation, sorrow and joy. In spite of all this, our lives are empty. Strip someone of position, power or money, and what are they? One had all that show outwardly but is empty and shallow inwardly. One cannot have both inner and outer riches. The inner fullness far outweighs the outer. One can be robbed of the outer; outer events shattering what has been carefully built up. But inner riches are incorruptible, nothing can touch them, for they have not been put together by the mind.

The more our life becomes improvised inside, the more we seek happiness outside. The inner riches that Krishnamurti speaks about are there for all of us to discover, but they require cultivation. This cultivation needs to take place in all dimensions of our life: physical, psychological, emotional, moral, and spiritual. Happiness is a three-legged stool comprising good health, meaningful work, and leisure. If one of these three legs is not securely placed, the edifice of our well-being will remain uneven and

---

[1] J. Krishnamurti, *Happy Is the One Who Is Nothing: Letters to a Young Friend* (Watkins, 2020), 39. Interestingly, Krishnamurti repeats these two lines on page 41 of the same book!

shaky. Workplaces that ensure a proper mix of these three constituents will reap the rewards in terms of less absenteeism, greater enthusiasm at work and an all-round affirmative work environment.

THE STOIC ART OF LIVING: STRATEGIES FOR THRIVING DURING TURBULENT TIMES[2]

During these challenging times, many have sought solace in Stoicism, a philosophy that has its roots in ancient Greece and Rome. It is a school of ancient Greco-Roman philosophy whose influence has persisted to the present day. It lays great emphasis on resilience and mental freedom gained from living a life of moral virtue in accordance with nature, thereby gaining a state of "imperturbable tranquility." It offers a deep philosophical framework and an ethical scaffold, especially relevant during hard times such as these. From Seneca, Epictetus to Marcus Aurelius during these early times to Victor Frankl and James Stockdale in our times, Stoicism has endured as a "tough-love" philosophy to live a fulfilling, meaningful life, even amidst adversity. The early Stoics learned all about managing crises, first-hand: they lived through exiles, wars, pandemics, and loss of loved ones.

Using universally applicable, rational principles to understand life, the Stoics devised various mind hacks that can be used to cope with stress, misfortune, and grief. Stoicism is especially an excellent philosophy for those in positions of power and leadership and for those in high-stress jobs. Additionally, Stoicism has inspired many modern approaches to personal development (such as "Self-Help" movement), influenced logotherapy and psychotherapy (in particular, cognitive behavioral therapy and its precursor, rational emotive behavior therapy). It is also popular with the US military and the National Health Services (NHS) in the UK.

---

[2] The following sections partially draw upon author's recent work: S. Dhiman, *More than Happiness: A Stoic Guide to Human Flourishing.* In S. Dhiman (ed.), *The Palgrave Handbook of Workplace Well-Being* (Cham: Palgrave Macmillan, 2021). https://doi.org/10.1007/978-3-030-02470-3_51-1.

STOIC PHILOSOPHY: POINTERS
FOR LIVING A FULFILLED LIFE

Philosophy does not promise to secure anything external for man, otherwise it would be admitting something that lies beyond its proper subject-matter. For as the material of the carpenter is wood, and that of statuary bronze, so the subject-matter of the art of living is each person's own life.
—Epictetus, *Discourses* 1.15.2, trans. Robin Hard (revised)[3]

For Epictetus, as for Socrates, as the above epigraph states, the proper study for the art of living is *examining* one's own life (cf. *Apology* 38a). The Stoics equated *eudaimonia* (flourishing) with virtue and recognized that happiness can be achieved through living a life of "value" (and not "valuables"); that is, by cultivating the four cardinal virtues of wisdom, courage, righteousness and self-control. Accordingly, Stoicism can provide us with best coping strategies to deal with the stress and maintain mental peace in a state of exception like a pandemic. It operates from two fundamental sets of axioms, by way of reminders to us: 1. It could be worse. 2. You are not the first one to experience this. 3. Worry and regret are irrational: If something is within your power to change, change it. Why regret or worry? If something is not within your power to change, then also why worry or feel regret. Armed with these three prompts, we can deal with all arrows and slings of outrageous fortune and circumstance with Stoic calm.

Additionally, Stoicism counters our general habit of complaining with the attitude of gratitude by reminding us that things could always be worse. As one writer put it: "Instead of complaining that you can't go to a concert, bar, or sporting event, be thankful that you do not have to go to the hospital" (Sullivan, 2021).[4] The Stoics also considered our duty to humanity takes precedence duty to oneself. What is good for the beehive is good for the bee. This simple understanding can help us to diligently

---

[3] Robin Hard, *Epictetus: Discourses, Fragments, Handbook,* trans. with an intro. and notes by Christopher Gill) (New York: Oxford University Press, 2014), 36.

[4] Bill Sullivan, Manage the Stress of COVID-19 with Stoicism: Psychological tools from the ancient Stoics can help you endure the pandemic. Psychology Today, January 5, 2021. Accessed: February 20, 2022: https://www.psychologytoday.com/us/blog/pleased-meet-me/202101/manage-the-stress-COVID-19-stoicism.

follow social distancing and using mask, etc. for the preservation of the greater good of the society.

During ancient times, philosophy was meant to provide a "design for living"—a set of rules to live one's life by. This ideal is nowhere realized with more urgency than Stoicism. Stoicism is a rational philosophy of life and its purpose is to help anyone live a better life. Christopher Gill, a pivotal figure in the revival of modern Stoicism, captures the essence of Stoic ethical self-development in the following "quick thumb-notes sketch" of the basic tenets of Stoicism:[5]

1. Our happiness is up to us. It does not depend upon acquiring material goods or career success but on developing the qualities that make us a good human being—that is, the cultivation of virtue.
2. We all have the innate capacity to generate our own happiness under all circumstances by developing the virtues.
3. If we do that, it will shape and determine over time our emotions and desires.
4. Stoics believe that we are naturally inclined to nurturing and caring relationships. What is different about Stoicism is that this is not just about our family and friends that we care for but humanity as a whole.
5. For Stoics, nature is not inert, materialistic—a fortuitous collection of atoms—but a living, organic whole of which we are a part. We exist as a part of nature as a whole and one of the key things to remember about nature is that nature is generous and providential and caring. And we should bear that in mind the way we live with nature.

According to Stoics, the principle—that we can achieve happiness or *eudemonia* by limiting our thoughts and actions to things under our control ("up to us") and accepting equanimously what are not ("not up to us")—encompasses all the wisdom needed to achieve happiness. The well-known "Serenity Prayer" generally attributed to Reinhold Niebuhr is thoroughly "Stoic":

---

[5] Christopher GillThe Five Principles of Stoicism. Retrieved March 3, 2019: https://player.fm/series/intellectual-explorers-club/christopher-gill-the-five-principles-of-stoicism.

God, grant me the serenity to accept the things I cannot change,
The courage to change the things I can,
And wisdom to know the difference.

It echoes Epictetus' observation that some things are under our control and some things are not. Wisdom lies in minding those things that are under our control and treating what we cannot control or change with equanimity or calm indifference.

STOIC EXERCISES: SURVIVORS' TOOLKIT

Stoicism is ideally suited for leadership development and the pursuit of well-being since it has its core as character, self-mastery, and purposeful action—the hallmarks of resilient leadership and flourishing. The life example of Admiral James Stockdale serves as a beacon of resilient leadership. Stockdale endured 7 1/2 years of extreme torture as naval POW in Hanoi Hilton, Vietnam, sustained by the teachings of Stoicism as his unassailable "inner citadel" and main survival kit.

Stoicism emphasizes that you can't control events, but you can control your responses to them. We present below four Stoic techniques/exercises to deal with the stress:

1. Dichotomy of Control: The Trump Card of Stoicism

One of the most robust psychological scaffolds that Stoics use is called "dichotomy of control": some things are in our control (our thoughts and actions) and some aren't (our health, property, reputation). The Stoic refrain: Focus on what is within your sphere of choice, and take the rest as it comes, with equanimity. The Stoic approach to eudaimonia hinges on understanding this distinction clearly. Whoever wants to be free, says Epictetus, should wish for nothing or avoid nothing that is up to other people (*Enchiridion*, 14).

By focusing on what is in our control and taking the rest as it comes with Stoic calm can go a long way in alleviating stress. What happens to us is never directly under my control, never completely up to us; however, our own thoughts and actions are. The pandemic is *not* really under my control—virus' mutation into various strands is not under my control—but the way I behave in response to it is in my control (wearing a mask, hand-sanitizing, practicing social distancing).

One of the basic psychological principles of Stoicism states that "It's not events that upset us but rather our judgment about them." More specifically, our judgment that something is really bad, or even catastrophic, causes our distress. Once understood in the right manner, it can brace us to deal with any adversity, including the post-COVID-19 environment, with Stoic calm.

2. View from the Above: Taking a Cosmic Perspective of Human Situation

This exercise consists of the act of reflecting on things from a larger perspective or taking a cosmic view of our human condition. In the grand scheme of things, everything is so small, so miniscule. Even our planet is a mere fraction of a dot! Seneca advises Lucilius in letter XCIX to "place before your mind's eye the vast spread of time's abyss, and embrace the universe; and then compare what we call human life with infinity."[6]

A variation of this exercise is to remember that we are not the first to experience adversity. Humanity endured several health pandemics such as cholera, the Spanish flu, and HIV/AIDS, to name just a few. Somehow, we do not seem to remember that in the past people have gone through such conditions as we ourselves have been since March 2020. Approached thus, we realize that things don't matter as much as or in the manner that we initially thought that they do. This practice enjoins us to look at external things dispassionately, not referring everything back to our own individual hopes and fears. Approaching life situations this way, we can preserve our tranquility, our most precious possession.

Marcus Aurelius refers to this practice at several places in his *Meditations* (e.g., IV.33, V.23, V.24). In this exercise, we strive to take a dispassionate view of our worldly concerns and weigh them in the cosmic scale: as the minute, passing, repetitive, and, in a word, "indifferent" affairs that they are, relative to the Stoic perspective for which virtue is the only true good.[7] Marcus Aurelius assures us that this view from the above will relieve us from the daily burdens of our human existence and

---

[6] Cited in Pierre Hadot, *Philosophy as a Way of Life* (Malden, MA: Blackwell, 1995), 182.

[7] See Pierre Hadot's Stoicism by Matthew Sharpe. Retrieved February 20, 2021: https://modernstoicism.com/pierre-hadots-stoicism-by-matthew-sharpe/.

foster a sense of wonder: Dwell on the beauty of life. Watch the stars, and see yourself running with them (*Meditations* VII.47).

This exercise is all about transcending one's individual perspective for a more total perspective that sages from all ages have bidden us. In his work *Human, All Too Human*, Friedrich Nietzsche, remembering Plato's words in the *Republic* (604c), says, "All in all, nothing in human affairs is worth taking very seriously, nevertheless."[8]

3. Memento Mori: The Finitude of Human Existence

This exercise is about reminding ourselves about the impermanence of things, relations, and events, including our own mortality. It said that in the ancient Rome, according to a practice hankering back to the more virtuous days of the Republic, Roman emperors had people whispering "*sic transit gloria mundi*" (worldly glories are fleeting) and "memento mori" (remember you are mortal) into their ears and their generals' ears during the parades and the chariot rides celebrating their triumphs.

Epictetus is succinct, "Continually remind yourself that you are a mortal being, and someday will die. This will inspire you not to waste precious time in fruitless activities, like stewing over grievances and striving after possessions."[9] This exercise is not about obsessively brooding over death all the time. Rather, it is about living urgently and authentically making the most with what we have in the time we have. It is about reminding ourselves how transient life yet precious life is and living it fully, without getting too attached to things, people, and positions. The moment we realize how fragile life is, we stop making "to-do" lists and start working on "to-be" list.

Apple's ex-CEO Steve Jobs' Stanford commencement speech, given 6 years before his death, was a moving meditation on mortality. He reminded the graduating class

---

[8] Friedrich Nietzsche, *Human, All Too Human: A Book for Free Spirits*, trans. by Marion Faber and Stephen Lehmann (Lincoln: University of Nebraska Press, 1996), 260.

[9] Sam Torode, *The Manual: A Philosopher's Guide to Life, a New Rendering* (CreateSpace Independent Publishing Platform, 2017), 25.

that "death is the destination we all share. No one has ever escaped it. And that is as it should be, because death is very likely the single best invention of life. It is life's change agent."[10]

Far from being morbid, frequently meditating on the finitude of our human existence could help us appreciate the time we have and make the most of life by becoming aware of its inherent fragility, precariousness, and preciousness.

4. Premeditatio Malorum: Negative Visualization

Negative visualization is a mental exercise—an experiment in imagination: we contemplate bad things so that we will be better prepared for them when they actually occur. The basic idea is to be prepared rather than sorry. Stoics use negative visualization to train themselves to stay calm and stay free from emotional anguish in the face of adversity. Also referred to as *premeditatio malorum* (literally, pre-meditating on future evils), this exercise is about imagining the worst that could happen. Why it is essential to practice negative visualization? Because whatever fate has given us, fate can take away without a moment's notice. The idea is not to make ourselves depressed. The idea is that contemplating these things in advance takes away their impact when they do happen.

As Seneca explains in his essay To Marcia on Consolation, ix.5, "He robs present ills of their power who has perceived their coming beforehand."[11] The very act of thinking about these things beforehand lessens their blow when such things happen. Seneca further explains that we should so brace ourselves beforehand through this practice that nothing ever takes us by surprise in letter XCI to his friend Lucilium:

> What is quite unlooked for is more crushing in its effect, and unexpectedness adds to the weight of a disaster. The fact that it was unforeseen has never failed to intensify a person's grief. This is a reason for ensuring that nothing ever takes us by surprise. We should project our thoughts ahead

---

[10] See Steve Jobs' 2005 Stanford Commencement Address (with intro by President John Hennessy). Retrieved February 16, 2021: https://www.youtube.com/watch?v1/4Hd_ptbiPoXM.

[11] Seneca, To Marcia on Consolation. In John W. Basore, trans., *Essays* Vol. II. Retrieved February 20, 2021: http://stoics.com/seneca_essays_book_2.html.

of us at every turn and have in mind every possible eventuality instead of only the usual course of events.[12]

That is why it is said that nothing happens to the wise person against his expectation. Such a person undertakes everything "with a reserve clause"... in his most steadfast decisions, he allows for uncertain events.[13] The wise person prefaces every under-taking with a reserve clause—"God willing" or "circumstances/fate permitting."

To summarize the Stoic perspective about dealing with adversity and living a life of fulfillment, the Stoic literature provides us with some good formulations of some "truths" to live by. We present one such formulation as follows:

1. Some things are within our control and some things are not.
2. We are not disturbed by events but by our opinions about them.
3. Life is what you make of it. It's up to you.
4. The universe is changing. Nothing lasts forever.
5. Do not act as if you had 10,000 years still to live...rather while you still can, while there is still time, make yourself good.

LIVING A LIFE OF FLOURISHING AND FULFILLMENT IS IN OUR OWN HANDS: POINTERS FOR LEADERS

As is evident from the foregoing, the Stoic approach is aimed at living a life that is impervious to external exigencies—"*the slings and arrows of outrageous fortune.*" As the great American historian Will Durant has observed in his exposition of the philosophy of Epictetus: "The essence of the matter is that a man should so mold his life that his happiness shall depend as little as possible upon external things."[14] External things are not within our control and pursuing them will make us vulnerable. "Who, then, is the invincible human being?" Epictetus once asked and answered the question himself: "One who can be disconcerted by nothing that lies

---

[12] Robin Campbell, Seneca, *Letters from a Stoic: Epistulae Morales Ad Lucilium*, selected and trans. with an intro. (UK: Penguin Classics, 2014), 205.

[13] Seneca cited in P. Hadot and M. Aurel, *The Inner Citadel: The Meditations of Marcus Aurelius* (Harvard University Press, 1998), 194.

[14] Will Durant, *The Story of Civilization: 3 Caesar and Christ* (New York: Simon and Schuster, 1972), 491.

outside the sphere of choice" (*Discourses* 1.18.21, tr. Robin Hard). Any misfortune "that lies outside the sphere of choice" should be considered an opportunity to strengthen our resolve, not an excuse to weaken it. This is one of the truly great mind hacks ever devised, this willingness to convert adversity to opportunity.[15]

Stoicism prepares us to deal with whatever happens by using the virtues that we have cultivated over many years. Stoics believe that our real good resides in our own character and virtuous actions. Happiness, they maintained, only depends on virtue, i.e., the mindset that makes you "do the right thing." And no one can truly take away this moral freedom from us. Victor Frankl writes in the manner of a Stoic: "Everything can be taken from a man but one thing: the last of the human freedoms—to choose one's attitude in any given set of circumstances, to choose one's own way."[16] This freedom to stay calm, to be good and to do good trumps all else in fostering happiness.

As free moral agents, we remain the masters of our fate and captains of our soul, to paraphrase William Ernest Henley.[17] Reminiscent of Victor Frankl, the following quote from Wolfe's novel underscores the ultimate freedom that we have, the freedom to assent to what is true and to deny what is untrue:

> One of the few freedoms that we have as human beings that cannot be taken away from us is the freedom *to assent to what is true* and *to deny*

---

[15] https://aeon.co/essays/why-stoicism-is-one-of-the-best-mind-hacks-ever-devised.

[16] Victor E. Frankl, *Man's Search for Meaning* (New York: Beacon Press, 2006), 66. This book, which has sold over 12 million copies worldwide, is a required reading for anyone looking for some proven pointers on the art of living meaningfully, under all conditions, including extreme unfavorable ones.

[17] See the last lines of *Invictus* by William Ernest Henley (Retrieved February 20, 2021: https://www.poetryfoundation.org/poems/51642/invictus):

> *It matters not how strait the gate,*
> *How charged with punishments the scroll,*
> *I am the master of my fate,*
> *I am the captain of my soul.*

what is false. Nothing you can give me is worth surrendering that freedom for.[18]

CONCLUDING REMARKS: BEING GRATEFUL FOR OUR SHARED DESTINY!

Stoics believe that we all have an inner sanctuary that we can retreat to and seek peace and freedom in the inner recesses of our soul. This "invulnerable fortress" (8.48)—"Inner Citadel"—is available to all of us to retreat to and to constantly renew ourselves. The art of living, Marcus Aurelius reminds us, is more like wrestling than dancing, for it requires that we should stand ready and firm to meet onsets which are sudden and unexpected (*Meditations*, 7.61, Hard, trans., slightly modified). When one sincerely lives the tenets of flourishing as shared in this chapter, one may feel like Seneca: *"I see in myself, Lucilius, not just an improvement but a transformation"* (Seneca, Moral Letters 6.1).

Epictetus reminds us that we can be grateful simply for our chance to play the part in the human drama and honor the profound mystery that we have together, our shared destiny. Humble and grateful, we can sing with Epictetus, "Wherever I go it will be well with me" (*Discourses*, 4.7.14). The wise person does everything in accordance with the spirit that dwells within and the Divine Will that fashions the universe. May we all be so fortunate!

---

[18] Tom Wolfe, *A Man in Full: A Novel* (New York: Farrar, Straus and Giroux; 1st edition, 1998), 671–672 [Emphasis added].

CHAPTER 2

Self-Transformation as a Prelude to Transform Organizations Based on the Ancient Traditions

Satish Modh

Abstract One is the friend of the self who has won over oneself; but one becomes enemy of oneself if one treats oneself like an enemy. As the Gita says one has to make an effort to constantly transform oneself in life without degrading oneself. If one can do this, it can help the self, the organization, and the work environment. The aim of this chapter is to provide a road map for self-transformation which can lead to transforming the organization. An effective organizational transformation cannot happen without self-transformation of those who are involved in leading the change. The self-transformation includes focusing on one's value system, strengthening one's resolve, dealing with people in the organization, and finally the work itself.

S. Modh (✉)
VES Institute of Management, Mumbai, India
e-mail: satish.modh@ves.ac.in

Keywords Self-transformation · Change · Organizational
Transformation · Organization culture

Uddharet ātmanātmānaṃ nātmānam avasādayet
ātmaiva hi ātmano bandhuh ātmaiva ripuh ātmana: | |Gita: 6.5| |

*Let one elevate oneself and not humiliate oneself. For, one is the friend of
oneself or, one is the enemy of oneself.*

INTRODUCTION

Organizations evolve continuously. To keep up with the fast paced
changes in technology, market, and environment they need to remain
agile, resilient, and flexible. Leaders who can bring this continual transformation have to anticipate future change and take people along by setting
their own example and remaining relevant (Ferry, 2022). The real change
is not a matter of transforming processes and technology; it is the people
in the organization who bring about a real transformation.

Self-transformation is the key to taking off. It is easier than to change
others. One can inspire, motivate, or influence others by one's own
example.

Lickerman (2012) writes, "Self-transformation means simply opening
our minds to something to which they've been closed. Even if we don't
know how we need to change, the simple act of looking inward with
a mind fully accepting of responsibility for strengthening what weakens
it finds and correcting what misconceptions it holds frequently yields
remarkable results."

Organizations are made of people—without people there is no organization. Business organizations serve people who are their customers and
stakeholders. It is important that people in the organizations truly understand their potential and work to satisfy their customers. While defining
management from ethical perspective, Modh (2017) writes:

> Management is a series of ethical actions done by people, using technology
> and resources, to achieve a state of joy and happiness in the minds of both,
> producers and customers.

In this new definition of management there are clear guidelines for people working in an organization. People in the organizations should perform ethical actions and work for attaining a state of joy and happiness in the minds of both, producers and customers. This definition is based on the theory of karma given in Mimansa—a Hindu text. This theory states that good actions produce good fruits and evil actions produce evil results. This theory implies that every individual should be guided by *karma yoga* which holds that "when duty is performed in a spirit of dedication it becomes the cause of freedom and liberation – freedom and liberation from sorrow." Morality, fair play, ethics, and justice are the basis of *karma yoga* (Adhikary, 2007). People seeking self-transformation follow the path of karma yoga and help greatly in transforming the organization.

SELF-TRANSFORMATION

Self-transformation is not just about adding positivity in one's life, it is also about taking care of stress and negative factors. Transformation is the beginning of a new understanding, one that is not contaminated with the present pessimism.

Transformation includes getting rid of habits one may want to change, such as smoking, drinking, or negative thought patterns and undesirable behaviors. Most of the time changing a habit is not a quick fix. It requires reprogramming of the mind, which takes place at the subconscious part of the mind. Therefore, it is important to understand the function and process of the mind, especially the subconscious mind. Human mind has three parts: conscious mind, subconscious mind, and super conscious mind (Kalra, 2013). The conscious mind is in charge of logic, reasoning, and voluntary actions such as reading, listening, writing, and speaking. Whatever we learn from reading and listening is recorded in our subconscious mind. The subconscious mind is the mind of the creativity, vision, and inventiveness. It stores and accumulates our learned behavior, beliefs, feelings, and memories. The super conscious mind is the spiritual part of the mind. It contains all feelings and emotions such as love, joy, harmony, persistence, compassion, kindness, truthfulness, tranquillity, and self-control as well as fear, sorrow, turbulence, anger, greed, and hatred.

For self-transformation one has to do a reality check—assess the state of one's body, mind, intellect, and what is the status of one's endurance in all the three. These basic means of functioning influences long-term interpersonal, organizational, and work-life balance issues. To begin the act of self-transformation, the following steps are needed:

1. Taking a reality check of one's personality.
2. Looking at one's value system—universal, social, cultural, or personal values.
3. Being self-aware to gain freedom from anger, lust, and greed.
4. Being conscious of one's actions, reasoning, and will power to do the right thing to gain health, prosperity, and happiness.

Self-transformation involves the transformation and purification of one's body, mind, and intellect which will create an awakening and strengthening of one's inner self (Scunziano-Singh, 2017).

The process of change requires training of all the three parts of the mind. It involves taking action with awareness and conscious efforts by training the conscious mind. It also involves taking action at the subconscious mind with positive feelings: The change takes place at the subconscious level with respect to one's behaviors or habits, annoying emotions or feelings. For such a self-transformation one has to do subconscious programming through pranayama, meditation, visualization, and other breathing techniques. All such changes start at the conscious mind, then subconscious mind, and finally the super conscious mind—spiritual mind. Self-transformation comes slowly and one has to have patience, it is a continuing improvement process. As Krishna tells Arjuna in the Bhagavad Gita:

Śanaiḥ śanairuparamēdbuddhyā dhṛtigṛhītayā |
ātmasaṃstham manaḥ kṛtvā na kiñchidapi chintayēt | |Gita 6.25| |

Slowly and slowly attain equanimity by the intellect held firm and the mind focussed within, not thinking of anything else.

Asaṃśayaṃ mahābāhō manō durnigrahaṃ chalam |
abhyāsēna tu kauntēya vairāgyēṇa cha gṛhyatē | |Gita 6.35| |

Undoubtedly the mind is fickle and restless, but by practice and self-restrain it can be disciplined.

According to Bhikkhu Bodhi (2022) the process of self-transformation involves the removal of objectionable mental dispositions and their substitution by pure attitudes conducing to the benefit of oneself and others. The principal stages of this gradual training are three: the training in virtue, the training in concentration, and the training in wisdom. In the Buddhist discipline faith could be compared with the seed of a tree, since it is faith that provides the initial impulse through which the training is taken up, and faith is the only thing that nourishes the training through every phase of the tree's development. Virtues are the roots, for it is virtue that gives grounding to our spiritual endeavors. Concentration is the trunk, the symbol of strength, and stability. Finally, wisdom are the branches, which yield the flowers of enlightenment and the fruits of freedom.

Obstacles in the Path of Self-Transformation

1. Weaknesses of the heart: Weakness of the heart comes at the most inappropriate time. At such moments one goes through anxiety, depression, and panic attack. Even the most capable people suffer from the weakness of the heart.
2. Confusion in the mind: There is confusion about the means and ends and ethical issues involved. Due to this most organizations should focus on an ethics program not just have a policy about it.
3. Sense enjoyment: This is the biggest hurdle. Everyone is tempted by money and sexual favors. Many top leaders have fallen prey to the greed and sexual harassment charges.
4. Response to success and failure: There is a clear tendency to overestimate oneself when successful and castigating oneself when faced with failure. One should deal with success and failure with equanimity.
5. Facing disruptive situations: In the era of fast innovations and changing technology there are disruptions all around. One has to learn to remain calm while facing any sort of disruptions.
6. Being aware of deception: One should be always aware of what is truth and what is false to remain aware of deception. The Gita says: "That which is false (*asat*) will not endure, while that which is true (*sat*) can never cease to exist. To the wise people, both these aspects of facts are obvious" (Gita 2:16).

Nāsatō vidyatē bhāvō nābhāvō vidyatē satah |
ubhayōrapi dṛṣṭō'ntastvanayōstattvadarśibhih | |Gita 2:16| |

It is important to train the intellect which gives one the power of discrimination to decide between what is right and what is wrong. An inept intellect is the biggest obstacle in the path of progress and cause of confusion. The Gita says:

Vyavasāyātmikā buddhirēkēha kurunandana |
bahuśākhā hyanantāścha buddhayō'vyavasāyinām | |Gita 2:41| |

A professional trained *buddhi* (intellect) is focussed and inept *buddhi* (intellect) keeps on deliberating on various views and positions.

When the intellect is inept and completely disillusioned, then one becomes indifferent to what is communicated and what is heard. Whereas, when the *buddhi* (intellect) becomes steady and unwavering, one is no longer distracted by what one hears. Once that happens, the subconscious mind, and super conscious mind becomes absorbed in *Samadhi* (meditative consciousness), and one is able to transform oneself.

Śrutivipratipannā tē yadā sthāsyati niśchalā |
samādhāvachalā buddhistadā yōgamavāpsyasi | |Gita 2:53| |

When your *buddhi* (intellect) remains steady and unwavering, you are no longer distracted by what you hear. Then, absorbed in *Samadhi* (meditative consciousness), you will be able to attain self-realization.

Those who are self-doubting and apprehensive are impelled by desires and are willing to do anything to get the results get trapped in the web of their desires leading to unrealistic expectations, misunderstandings, deep disappointments, and broken relationships (Gita 5:12). Therefore, it is important to restrain the mind and intellect to be on the path of self-transformation.

Indicators for Progress Toward Self-Transformation

Bhagavad Gita chapter 2 verses 55 to 60 explains in detail about a person who has mastered the body, mind, and intellect and is able to restrain the impulses of desires and temperaments. Such people have following qualities:

1. When people give up all desires of the mind and are self-satisfied and contented
2. Whose mind is not agitated in sorrow, and remains indifferent in joy
3. Those who are free from attachment, fear, and anger
4. Who are without likes and dislikes
5. Who are not jubilant in gain, and are not dejected in loss
6. Who are able to withdraw their senses from the sense objects in all situations, as a tortoise draws in its limbs

TRANSFORMING PEOPLE BEFORE TRANSFORMING THE ORGANIZATION

Organizations are living entities. Transformation of organization is a continuous improvement process involving people in the organization. You need to transform the mindsets and behavior of people in the organization. When you are asking others to transform it is important to begin the process with yourself.

It is likely that not everyone in the organization is able to understand what you want and is unable to keep pace with you. How to deal with them? The Gita says:

Na buddhibhēdaṃ janayēdajñānāṃ karmasaṅginām |
jōṣayētsarvakarmāṇi vidvānyuktaḥ samācharan | |Gita 3:26| |

Wise people should not create conflict in the mind of ignorant people who are attached to results of *karma*. They should inspire them by performing their own *karma* diligently.

Further, a person on the path of self-transformation does not differentiate between people who are with him, or opposed to him, or neutral to him. This is the key to the transformation process. The Gita says:

Suhṛnmitrāryudāsīnamadhyasthadvēṣyabandhuṣu |
sādhuṣvapi cha pāpēṣu samabuddhirviśiṣyatē | |Gita 6:9| |

One who gives the same attention to the good-hearted, friends, enemies, the indifferent, the neutral, the hateful, the relatives, the righteous and the unrighteous, he excels.

Such a person is continuously aware of key people in the transformation process. He keeps on tracking their contribution: Is this individual aware of what one must do to make the transformation succeed? Is it clear to them what will happen if they don't participate in the process? Have I given them a chance to be part of the process? Have I been able to present myself as a role model for others to change their mindsets and behavior?

This approach would have a positive impact on the people in the organization. Those who are with you become more motivated, those who are not with you don't obstruct the process, and those who are hesitant start realizing that they need to be more active. This approach has to be followed relentlessly to succeed.

Organizations are made up of various systems and processes. These systems and processes are the life line of people who work in the organization and they are difficult to change. Every process and process owner will fight tooth and nail to keep it the way it is. Therefore, it is important to change the mindsets of people. The key to success is to deal with the process owner and make him or her understand the transformation process.

It is not as easy as it sounds. Many process owners will fail to understand your view point. If you don't bring them on board the whole transformation process would falter. The question is: Why do people resist change?

According to the *Samkhya* School, the universe is made from three *Gunas*, called *Sattva*, *Rajas*, and *Tamas*. The Sanskrit term *"Guna,"* in its ordinary sense, means the "quality" or "energies" or "characteristics" of nature. *Sattva* (S) defines goodness—the energy that is "spiritual" in nature. *Rajas* (R), on the other hand, is concerned with passionate action—the emotional energy that drives action. *Tamas* (T), in a similar vein, is associated with inertia—the inertia of the body—i.e., the resistance to change. These three energies are eternally bound to one another and are in a constant state of flux; they each try to overpower, support, produce, and intimately mix with one another. These energies and their interactions with each other influences the way we work. This is presented in the Fig. 2.1.

Primary energies:

1. Spiritual energy (S): It is your *spirituality* that inspires one's understanding of goodness, truth, purity, and knowledge through reason and perception.
2. Emotional energy (R): Your *emotions* and their intensity provide the energy to realize a cause, or pursue an interest, or fulfill a purpose in life.
3. Potential energy—Inertia (T): It is the stored energy of your physical body—your present state. It is also linked with the *inertia*—the

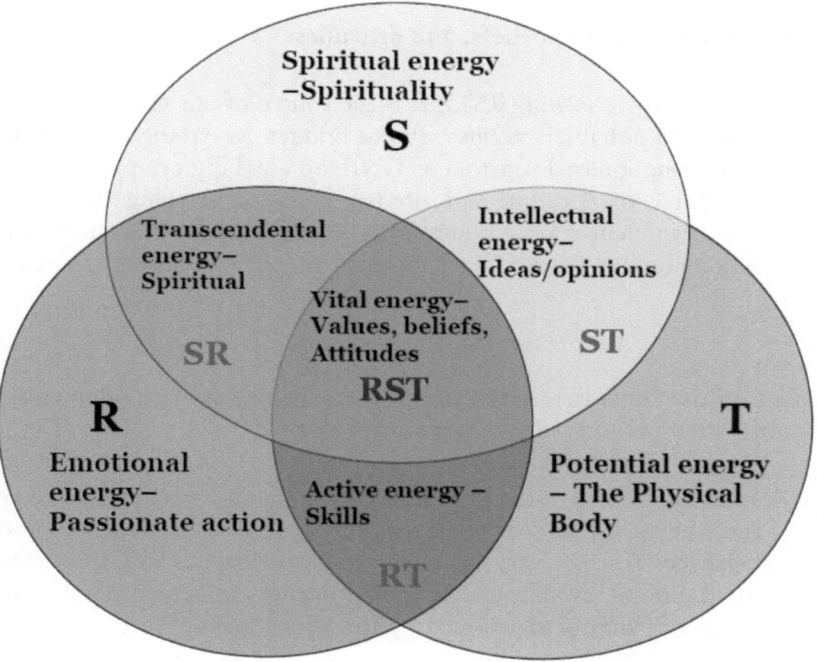

Fig. 2.1 Seven energies that drive your personality

power of resistance through which everybody tries to preserve their status quo.

Composite energies:

1. Transcendental energy (RS): the combination of your spiritual and emotional energies. It drives your *spiritual emotions* which determines your focus on worldly, religious, and virtuous actions.
2. Active energy (RT): The combination of your emotional and potential energies. It drives your *physical activity* which determines how physically energetic are you. Your energetic efforts have a direct influence on your skill-set.
3. Intellectual energy (ST): It is the combination of your spiritual and potential energies. It drives your *mental activity* which influences your mind in the pursuits of learning, research, and innovation.

Key energy: Values, beliefs, and attitudes

1. Vital energy—*Prana* (RST): It is the source of our emotional, spiritual, and potential energies. *Prana* bridges everything external and everything internal together as ONE. So anything even your breath is capable of affecting and altering every other thing. Your vital energy influences your values, beliefs, and attitudes that shape your actions toward yourself, one another, the planet, and the universe.

Resistance to Change

Based on the Guna theory the resistance to change could be due to five factors, based on your true nature.

1. You may believe in the importance of individual freedom. You may take the view that society or religion should not impose a code of behavior. You are very liberal in your worldview. You are willing to ignore or even spurn religious norms, accepted morals, and forms of behavior sanctioned by the larger society. You are flexible and adaptable to new things. You may have very low resistance to change.

2. You may have the ability to change yourself so as to live up to social and other standards. You may have will power to remain in control of situations and surroundings, but you live by self-discipline and responsibility. Your self-discipline keeps you rooted to your way of life. You are a confident, disciplined, and orderly person. Your resistance to change could be due to the importance given to your own personal value systems and memories.

3. You may love to lead a routine life. You are grounded, salt-of-the-earth types. You do not feel strongly one way or the other. You tend to act without prejudice or compulsion which may also be taken as apathy, indifference, or a lack of conviction. You resist change due to your habits, predetermined reaction to certain situations, or emotions. You are resistant to change due to your life style, customs, and traditions. You may resist change because you want to go through the overall process framework. You resist change also because it is difficult to change your habits.

4. You may be more comfortable when you maintain status quo. Your views and opinions once created are difficult to change. You are not prone to changes—you stick to what you have known. You want to continue on the current trajectory of your life. It gives you a sense of security and well-being. Moreover, you don't have enough motivation to change from the current state of affairs.

5. You may present yourself as a challenging mountain which is difficult to conquer. Sometimes, you can be unbelievably stubborn and inflexible in your approach. You have lot of hidden talent which is not yet actualized. You have good strength and high potential. You might have nearly accepted your current situation as your true destiny. While you could be patient, you could also be lazy, especially when ordered to do something. You will not move a muscle till you are motivated to get up and work.

A person who is on the path of self-transformation understands these variations in the nature and behavior of people and acts based on the true understanding of human nature. The Guna theory helps in understanding not only one's own mindset and behavior but that of others too. This shows just *how* difficult the process of change could be. To move the process of transformation smoothly in the organization, there is a need to make people aware of their personalities. Mostly these are the reasons for not being able to bring everyone on board:

- Lack of training or preparation for people in the organization
- An organizational culture not ready to adapt to change
- Lack of a transformation strategy
- Lack of a roadmap to the transformation process
- People leading the change are not on the path of self-transformation

The Table 2.1 gives a summary of seven energies, their attributes, and influences.

Table 2.1 The seven energies, their attributes, and influences

Energy	Attribute	Influence
Spiritual energy (S)	Spirituality	It influences us toward goodness, truth, purity, and knowledge through reason and understanding
Emotional energy (R)	Passionate action	It provides emotional energy for action to realize a cause, or pursue an interest or fulfill a purpose in life
Potential energy (T)	Inertia	The physical body and its power of resistance to preserve the present state
Transcendental energy (RS	Spiritual emotions	Spiritual emotion is basically a state of experiencing the Divine within ourselves and others
Intellectual energy (RT)	Ideas/opinions	It influences our capacity for imagination, recognition, and appreciation, and is also responsible for processing feelings and emotions
Active energy (ST)	Skills	This energy builds our essential skills (communication, etc.), work skills (domain specific), and life skills (Interpersonal)
Vital energy (RST)	Values, beliefs, attitudes	Also called "*Prana*"—this influences our values, beliefs, and attitudes. It shapes our actions toward ourselves, one another, the planet, and the universe

ORGANIZATIONAL TRANSFORMATION

Organizational transformation is an organization's need to adapt to the external environment by changing itself.

Organizational transformation is not an incremental change. It does not tackle few areas in the organization but goes for a complete system and process overhaul. Organizational transformation touches the people and culture, the processes, technologies, structures, and governance mechanism.

The need for change arises from the desire to equip the organization for the future. Some of the issues are:

- Realigning the organization structure with its operations
- Reforming the company culture
- Transforming the operating environment
- Incorporating new technology and digital transformation
- Expansion and growth
- Developing the leadership team

The need for organizational transformation may arise due to:

- Changes in the external environment
- Improving internal processes and systems
- New opportunities
- Improving efficiency and effectivity

The first thing to be done is to formulate a vision of the future. Based on this vision one has to look at the mission statements and values of the organization. What are the goals and objectives of the organization?

There are various models which are available for organizational transformation, one of them is the congruence model (Nadler & Tushman, 1980). This model looks at the organizational functioning and develops a process for analyzing organizational problems. It is a tool, that may be useful for structuring the complexity of organizational life and helping managers create, maintain, and develop effective organizations. The congruence model breaks the organization itself into four elements that, when aligned will facilitate change:

- Work—the series of tasks required to perform each function
- People—who perform the tasks
- Existing organizational structures, processes, and practices—specifications on how work is assigned and performed
- Informal organization—daily interactions between people within the organization and customers

Organizational Culture and the Readiness for Change

Organizational culture is a system of values, beliefs, and behavior patterns which subconsciously drives members of the organization to make each choice and decision (Ortega-Parra & Sastre-Castillo, 2013). An excellent organizational culture includes motivated employees and value-driven management (Pathiranage et al., 2020). The involvement of the employees in the organizational decision-making process is critical for enhancing performance (Miguel, 2015). When engaged in the organizational decision-making process, employees may build a sense of ownership and obligation (Engelen et al., 2014). As employees build a culture of ownership and obligation, their loyalty and commitment toward the organization increases substantially even without close supervision (Denison, 1990; Nwibere, 2013).

There is a resistance to change due to the comfort of existing systems and processes. Managing resistance to change is the number one area of concern in the organizational transformation process. The belief that people resist change due to the organizational culture may not be exactly true. Even when there is no visible resistance to change, people may not be ready to participate in the transformation process. What is needed is to create an atmosphere of adaptability and openness. That is possible when people in the organization are aware of their own self-transformation. Self-transformation of people in the organization has to be considered as a prelude to the transformation process. When people will move toward self-transformation they will willingly participate in organizational transformation. The following steps are needed to expedite the process:

1. An environment of openness where people can give and receive feedback without any repercussions.

2. People in the organization should be encouraged to participate in spiritual practices, e.g., yoga, breathing exercises, meditation. This will help them in being aware of their own self.
3. Need to overcome biases toward others and having faith that most of the people are willing to change.
4. Leaders have to lead by example and become role model for others.
5. Understand one's own true nature that will help in understanding others as well.
6. Create processes to get people actively involved in organizational transformation.

The above steps would help in creating the culture of change and people will be ready to participate with full commitment.

Importance of Change Management in Organizational Transformation

Organizational transformation involves organizational change. Therefore, change management is important when it comes to organizational transformations. Such a change management process would include:

- A project management approach
- Risk evaluation and mitigation
- Making people aware
- Seeking support of people in the transformation process

One should be aware that change happens at the individual level. In order for an organization to change, all the individuals within the organization must change. When communicating to people about the organizational transformation effort:

- They should be informed about the policy, purpose, and process of the change project.
- They should be informed about the responsibilities, duties, and accountability systems.
- Opinions of people should be heard with an open mind.

ATTRIBUTES OF A PERSON WITH SELF-REALIZATION

How do we know that person is progressing well on the path self-transformation. Self-transformation is a continuous process of self-improvement and self-realization. The Gita gives some of the qualities of such a person. One has to look within and discover whether some of these qualities are being inculcated. The Gita says:

- **Maintaining equilibrium**: "The one who is self-restrained, self-realized and peaceful maintains equilibrium in cold and heat, pleasure and pain, as also in honour and dishonour" (Gita 6:7).
- **Self-restrained**: "One who is acquainted with suitable empirical and scientific knowledge, who has won over *indriya* (sense organs) and is spiritually inclined, such a contemplative person (*yukta*) is called a *yogi* - who treats alike a lump of earth, a stone and gold" (Gita 6:8).
- **Treating everyone equally**: "One who gives the same attention to the good-hearted, friends, enemies, the indifferent, the neutral, the hateful, the relatives, the righteous and the unrighteous, stands out" (Gita 6:9).
- **Without attachment**: "Let the *yogis* try to remain steady by always remaining in solitude, with their mind and intellect focussed, free from desires and without the sense of possession." (Gita 6:10). "Those who are established in *yoga*, with purity of consciousness, self-controlled, self-restrained, all inclusive (identifies oneself with everyone), do not get attached to actions (Gita 5:7)
- **Feeling of I am not the doer**: "People who know the truth believe, 'I don't do anything, thus' while seeing, hearing, touching, smelling, eating, moving, sleeping or breathing, speaking, releasing, taking, opening and closing eyes, thus convinced that the senses move amongst the sense objects" (Gita 5:8–9).

RESPECT THE WORK YOU ARE DOING

In the process of organizational transformation, it is very important that people respect the work they are doing. If they are not happy with what they are doing, there will be stress and unhappiness and they will not do their work efficiently and effectively. A person who is on the path of self-transformation understands that there is no work small or big, or, more important than what they are doing. The Gita says:

sreyan sva-dharmo vigunah para-dharmat sv-anusthitat
sva-dharme nidhanam sreyahpara-dharmo bhayavahah | |Gita 3.35| |

It is better to do your own *Karma*, however lacking in importance, than to do that of another, even though looking glamorous. It is better to even die doing one's own *Karma*, since performing someone else's *Karma* has serious consequences.

śhreyān swa-dharmo vigunaḥ para-dharmāt sv-anuṣhṭhitāt
svabhāva-niyatam karma kurvan nāpnoti kilbiṣham | |Gita 18:47| |

It is better to do one's own *karma*, even though imperfectly, than to do another's *karma* perfectly. By doing one's *karma*, a person does not suffer any harm.

saha-jam karma kaunteya sa-doṣham api na tyajet
sarvārambhā hi doṣheṇa dhūmenāgnir ivāvṛitāḥ | |Gita 18:48| |

One should not abandon one's own *karma*, even if one sees shortcomings in them, O *Kaunteya*. As fire is hidden by smoke, similarly all activities have some hidden unpleasant element.

DISCUSSION

Your true nature defines you, your natural tendencies, and core values. Every person has these qualities whether one is aware or not. Recognizing those values can define the nature of your work and your contribution to the organization. The path of self-transformation will make you aware of that. You will discover your work based on your true nature and you will take pride in what you are doing. Modh (2018) has developed a framework based on the concept of Guna to ascertain the true nature of a person. One can give the test on the website and find out one's personality (true nature) based on Triguna. When everyone in the organization takes pride in their work the process of organizational transformation becomes that much smooth.

You can also recognize your organization's core values and why they matter. With this appreciation, you can now decide how you will contribute in the whole process of organizational transformation, sometimes going beyond the call of your duty.

Many a times you question the worth of your job and your contribution, but once you know that you are part of a process and every part is important in the whole process you would start respecting your own part and your contribution. You can also share your experiences with others and encourage them to follow this approach.

You can never be happy if you don't take pride in your work and are not proud of the place where you work. Taking pride in our work and the organization helps in feeling good, motivates you, and finally helps in self-transformation while contributing to the organizational transformation.

REFERENCES

Adhikary, N. M. (2007). *Mimamsa-philosophy and mass media ethics.* BODHI an Interdisciplinary Journal. Department of Languages and Mass Communication.

Bodhi, B. (2022). *Self-transformation through right living.* Hinduwebsite.Com. Retrieved August 10, 2022, from https://hinduwebsite.com/buddhism/ess ays/nourishing_roots.asp

Denison, D. R. (1990). *Corporate culture and organizational effectiveness.* Wiley.

Engelen, A., Flatten, T., Thalmann, J., & Brettel, M. (2014). The effect of organizational culture on entrepreneurial orientation: A comparison between Germany and Thailand. *Journal of Small Business Management, 52,* 732–752.

Ferry, K. (2022, January 26). *Organizational transformation.* Korn Ferry. Retrieved August 10, 2022, from https://www.kornferry.com/insights/fea tured-topics/organizational-transformation

Kalra, S. (2013, May 29). *The secret of self-transformation: How to change your behavior one step at a time.* Speakingtree.In. Retrieved August 10, 2022, from https://www.speakingtree.in/blog/the-secret-of-selftransformation

Lickerman, A. (2012). *The undefeated mind: On the science of constructing an indestructible self* (1st ed.). Health Communications Inc EB.

Modh, S. (2017). *Ethical management* (2nd ed.). Trinity Press.

Modh, Satish. (2018). *Triguna yoga.* Retrieved August 29, 2022, from https://www.satishmodh.com/

Miguel, P. C. (2015). Receiving a national quality award three times: Recognition of excellence in quality and performance. *The TQM Journal, 27,* 63–78.

Nadler, D. A., & Tushman, M. L. (1980). A model for diagnosing organizational behavior. *Organizational Dynamics, 9*(2), 35–51.

Nwibere, B. (2013). The influence of corporate culture on managerial leadership style: The Nigerian experience. *International Journal of Business and Public Administration, 10,* 166–187.

Ortega-Parra, A., & Sastre-Castillo, M. (2013). Impact of perceived corporate culture on organizational commitment. *Management Decision, 51,* 1071–1083.

Pathiranage, Y. L., Jayatilake, L. V., & Abeysekera, R. (2020). A literature review on organizational culture towards corporate performance. *International Journal of Management, Accounting and Economics, 7*(9), 522–544.

Scunziano-Singh, M. (2017, August 30). *The power of change: Self-transformation and leading a more fulfilling life in an uncomplicated way.* Wellcome Om Integral Healing & Education Center. Retrieved August 10, 2022, from https://wellcomeomcenter.com/power-change-self-transformation-leading-fulfilling-life-uncomplicated-way/

CHAPTER 3

Mindfulness in Mexican Organizations: An Effective Way to Increase Individual and Organizational Well-Being

*Laura E. Garza-Meza, Luis Portales,
and Nancy E. Westrup-Villarreal*

Abstract In this chapter, the authors present a study of mindfulness in Mexican organizations as an effective way to increase individual and organizational well-being. It presents the benefits perceived on a personal and organizational level by employees of two different organizations that have mindfulness programs. The creation of these programs within their respective organizations took different paths; while in one organization the impulse and creation came from top management, in the

L. E. Garza-Meza (✉) · L. Portales · N. E. Westrup-Villarreal
Universidad de Monterrey, San Pedro Garza García, Mexico
e-mail: laura.garza@udem.edu

L. Portales
e-mail: luis.portales@udem.edu

N. E. Westrup-Villarreal
e-mail: nancy.westrup@udem.edu

S. Dhiman (ed.), *New Horizons in Workplace Well-Being*,
https://doi.org/10.1007/978-3-031-17241-0_3

other, middle managements created the mindfulness programs. The study followed a qualitative approach, with the interest of recovering the voice of the participants and knowing these benefits in greater depth. In the first section, the authors present a brief review of mindfulness construct and its origins. It briefly presents the Mexican context in which the interviews were conducted, as well as the characteristics of the interviewees. The third section presents the results of mindfulness on a personal level, how the collaborators see it and how they apply it in their day-to-day lives. The fourth section presents the results at the organizational level, according to several dimensions.

Keywords Mindfulness · Organizational Well-being · Mexican Organizations

INTRODUCTION

Mindfulness has a positive effect on all the social facets of the people who practice it, including those carried out in their professional life.
   —Authors

The study of spirituality in organizations gained its relevance in recent decades. Although the first approximate date from the nineteenth century of the work done by the chaplains in the battlefields (Damore et al., 2004), it was until the end of the twentieth century that its study became relevant, especially by the relationship between performance of collaborators and organizations as a whole (Hicks, 2003; Krishnakumar & Neck, 2002; Zinnbauer et al., 1999).

According to Ashmos and Duchon (2000), his entry into organizational theory had its origin in the organizational changes that occurred during the eighties and nineties, which were characterized by mergers, constant restructuring, and mass layoffs. These changes hurt people's mental health and social life. Also, this entry was accompanied by the impulse from a conceptual perspective of organizational change models that included spiritual elements, consolidating it as an alternative to deal with these new circumstances (Pérez Santiago, 2007).

The concern to manage spirituality in the business world produced new programs which were designed in various organizations offering special tools or methods that favored their results, their benefits were eventually discovered, especially the relationship between the general well-being of their workers and the impact this had on the productivity of their organization. (Portales, 2015; Portales & Garza-Meza, 2016).

Among the programs or methods that have most quickly positioned themselves in recent years are those related to the concept of mindfulness, which consists of being intentionally aware of what is done, without judging, adhering, or rejecting in any way the experience (Zivnuska et al., 2016). The practice of mindfulness in organizations has certain benefits, mainly individual, especially those related to stress management and the conditions of uncertainty to which employees are on a day-to-day basis (Hülsheger et al., 2013; Roth & Stanley, 2002); and at the organizational level with the improvement of culture, responsibility, and learning (Cacioppe, 2017).

The studies carried out in the field of mindfulness in organizations, focused on analyzing the impact that these programs have on individual and organizational levels separately, which is a fact that opened the opportunity to generate approaches that consider a multilevel perspective (Sutcliffe et al., 2016), The adoption of a multilevel approach allowed the possibility of being able to identify the benefits generated integrally in the collaborators, the organization and even toward third parties, as is the case of the family and the group of friends.

The study of mindfulness within companies and the perceived impacts on collaborators have mainly focused on developed countries. However, there is little work carried out in developing countries (Ogliastri & Zúñiga, 2016). In these countries, the problems associated with occupational stress have acquired serious dimensions, such as in México where 75% of its employees have burnout syndrome or fatigue due to work stress. China has a slightly lower level with 73%, and the USA has 59% (Forbes, 2017). It is important to mention that in Mexico different companies and organization from different sectors have begun to implement mindfulness programs since they are interested in addressing this problem and the consequences it generates, such as absenteeism, low productivity, and work accidents, among others (Siegrist, 2001; Siegrist & Wahrendorf, 2016).

Based on this context, this chapter presents the benefits perceived on a personal and organizational level by employees of two different organizations that have mindfulness programs. The creation of these programs within their respective organizations took different paths; while in one organization the impulse and creation came from top management, in the other, middle managements created the mindfulness programs. The study followed a qualitative approach, with the interest of recovering the voice of the participants and knowing these benefits in greater depth.

The chapter is structured in four sections; the first section presents a brief review of what mindfulness is, its origins and change in perception at the moment of operationalizing it. The second one briefly presents the Mexican context in which the interviews were conducted, as well as the characteristics of the interviewees. The third section presents the results of mindfulness on a personal level, how the collaborators see it and how they apply it in their day-to-day lives. The fourth section presents the results at the organizational level, according to several dimensions. Both in the individual and the organizational analysis, an analysis model was generated. Finally, the last part presents a summary of the chapter and its central elements.

A Brief Review of Mindfulness in Organizations

Mindfulness is the translation of the Pali language in which Buddha's teachings were initially recorded into English from the word "sati," which refers to a sense of awareness attention, and remembrance (Siegel et al., 2009). Within the Buddhist tradition, there are various understandings about this practice; however, all of them have as common elements the purpose and function of offering attention meditation practices for psycho-spiritual development (Purser & Milillo, 2014).

In terms of purpose, the practice of mindfulness focuses on eliminating unnecessary suffering by cultivating the perception of the functioning of the mind and the nature of the material world (Dunne, 2015). At a meditative training level in depth, it alleviates and eliminates suffering by inducing significant and sustainable changes in cognitive and emotional states, which lead to dramatic and irreversible changes in psychological behavior (Brown et al., 2007). This process of psycho-spiritual development involves a meditative and contemplative path of inquiry aimed at identifying and transforming the fundamental causes of suffering (Purser & Milillo, 2014; Rupprecht et al., 2018).

Buddhist meditative practices embodied awareness and the cultivation of clarity, emotional balance (equanimity), and compassion, capacities that can be refined and developed through the intentional unfolding of attention; reason for which it can be considered as universal (Dorjee, 2010; Siegel et al., 2009). That is, no matter what religion the practitioner professes or the culture from which he comes from, he can carry out mindfulness processes whenever he chooses. This universality opened the door to its introduction and positioning in conventional, secular environments with the interest in reducing suffering and mental states and behaviors that compose it, such as psychology of health care and general care (Dunne, 2015; Segal et al., 2013; Williams & Kabat-Zinn, 2011).

The positioning of mindfulness in the West, mainly in the USA, was in the seventies when Kabat-Zinn generated a program of stress reduction that included a daily meditation and self-awareness exercises, with techniques used in cognitive behavioral therapy (Kabat-Zinn, 2003). The implementation of this type of programs oriented to the use of the practice of mindfulness from a functional and objective perspective, and using therapeutic and behavioral elements of western psychology, left aside the religious and cultural roots of Buddhism that promote compassion and lighting (Shapiro et al., 2006).

This program developed other therapeutic models based on mindfulness, such as Mindfulness-Based Cognitive Therapy (MBCT), which consists of an 8-week program that combines Kabat-Zinn's proposal with other aspects of conductive theory, by accepting their thoughts and feelings without any judgment and focusing on the present (Kuyken et al., 2008; Segal et al., 2013).

The results obtained with the start-up as a therapeutic element in the area of psychology led companies to start implementing mindfulness programs in their interior. Within the framework of these programs, mindfulness at work can be defined as a psychological state in which employees pay full attention to the present moment while performing tasks, with the interest of generating a benefit for the organization and the employee (Zivnuska et al., 2016).

Research on mindfulness at work shows that employees not only increase their organizational performance (Pang & Ruch, 2019) and a higher level of engagement (Tuckey et al., 2018). They also change aspects of their daily life, such as the fact that they have better stress management and better control of their emotions on a day-to-day basis (Hülsheger et al., 2013. Another impact that mindfulness programs have shown is that employees perceive greater well-being in their work and their daily life (Dorjee, 2010; Pinck & Sonnentag, 2018; Slutsky et al., 2018, Zivnuska, et al, 2016).

In this way, mindfulness breaks into organizational practice, not with the interest of eliminating unnecessary suffering by meditation practices, but with the idea to increase the perception of well-being perceived by the collaborators, given a more functionalist perspective. This situation has been criticized by some scholars and practitioners of this type of techniques, who emphasize the fact that the practice of mindfulness has been inserted within the neoliberal and consumerist paradigm, leaving aside the purpose of this Buddhist practice (Hyland, 2017; Walsh, 2017).

Birth of Organizational Mindfulness in a Stressed Society with Little Security

The arrival of mindfulness in the organizational sphere has not been exclusive of developed countries or large corporations, but has also been permeating developing countries where organizational stress is an epidemic and where insecurity or social instability are constant, as is the case of Mexico where most of the chronic diseases that Mexican society suffers are triggered by the pressure and work stress (Rodríguez Zárate, 2018).

In this line, the labor depression defined as a feeling of deep sadness, discouragement, and a great generalized lack of energy associated with work (Cruz, 2018), is a cause of the leading causes of work disability in this country (Velázquez & Lino, 2018). The labor depression generated an impact of 1.2 million dollars during 2017, impacting 7,000 workers of which 60% were women (Mejía, 2018). One of the characteristics of the type of depression is that no matter the job, age, or social status, any worker may have this depressive disorder.

In this context, Mexican companies and organizations have begun to offer mindfulness programs inside. Some of them have driven it from top management, making it mandatory to participate in the leaders of the company, as a way to reduce stress and improve their perception of well-being. In other companies, middle managers have opted for a voluntary scheme for their employees, and have developed by the request who seek to obtain part of their benefits.

Twelve in-depth interviews were carried out with the interest of evidence of the personal and organizational benefit that the practice of mindfulness generated by the collaborators of two organizations. These two organizations were selected because the origin of the mindfulness programs were different. The first one is Daltile, a global Company dedicated to the manufacture of ceramic products; and the second one is the University of Monterrey (UDEM) a private university in Nuevo León. For both institutions, the care and development of their human capital are critical, both declaring them in their organizational values.

At Daltile, mindfulness training started from the company's presidency, and it was the president who invited his next level to support it by participating actively. OIn contrast, UDEM began its experience in a different manner when its Center for Teacher Development and Innovation ("Centro de Innovación y Desarrollo"—CID) began by offering its teachers and other collaborators to participate. The interviewees were people trained with the mindfulness methodology who dedicated different numbers of hours per week and who had between one and four years of practice (Table 3.1).

Of the UDEM collaborators, 6 of the 8 were professors and 2 were an administrative staff of the CID, all of them arrived at the workshop without much information about what mindfulness was, but also everyone was looking for tools to feel better. Alejandra recalls: "I was going through a personal situation and I did not know about mindfulness, so I started with yoga, and they offered me the course of mindfulness … it was like just in time." On the other hand, the directors of Daltile, although they attended the workshop by invitation, most were skeptical and without much information, but open to learning. For example, Edgar mentions ".... skepticism at the beginning and conviction at the end, to the extent of continuing to practice."

For the interviewees, mindfulness has to do with taking a few minutes of the day to stop and return to the present mind, to full attention, as mentioned by Luis Eugenio: "It is about giving me a few minutes a day, as to focus, locate myself, how I am, where I am, emotionally, a little too, as well as an almost therapeutic aspect… to put things in their place, and principle one would assume that those minutes will serve me as to face the slopes I have, the moments I have during the day."

For his part for Adris is: "I see it as seeing myself, how to recognize myself, how to give me space, how to pay attention." For Alejandra it is "… remembering to live in the present" and for Eduardo, it is "Primarily, it is meditation."

Table 3.1
Classification of interviewees by company, years of practice, and time dedicated to the practice of mindfulness

Organization	Name	Years of practice	Dedication time
DALTILE	Confidential	1	10 min daily
DALTILE	Jesús Ortega	3	15 min twice a week
DALTILE	Edgar Hernández	2	15 min three times a week
DALTILE	Eduardo Rodríguez	3	10 min three times a week
UDEM	Adriana Estrada	4	15 min daily
UDEM	Karina Gómez	2	20 min daily
UDEM	Anais Flores	4	10 min once a week
UDEM	Adris Díaz	4	30 min three times a week
UDEM	Luis Eugenio Espinoza	4	15 min four times a week
UDEM	Josefina Ibarra	3	30 min four times a week
UDEM	Alejandra Galindo	2	60 min daily
UDEM	Guadalupe Siller	4	20 min four times a week

Source Authors

PERSONAL BENEFITS PERCEIVED

The benefits perceived by the interviewees were physical, cognitive, emotional, and, to a lesser degree, spiritual. The most important physical benefit shared by all associated with their practice of mindfulness was not only the reduction of their stress, but most of all that it reduced or eliminated their chronic diseases. All the interviewees mentioned that the stress decreased and with this, they improved their health.

Luis Eugenio commented: "… for more than two and a half years, I no longer have gastritis, when I used to have severe periods of this."

Guadalupe shared, "…mindfulness courses create neutral connections so to mention our gastritis, colitis, migraine, have disappeared from our vocabulary."

For one of the directors of Daltile, the benefit also focuses on the prevention and listening of the body. He mentioned: "It helps you to listen more to your body; it talks to you too much, and suddenly when you eat things the next day and you have a swollen stomach, you reflect…it allows you to read your body and know your body."

Josefina commented: "I feel more relaxed…I changed by eating habits…I had diagnosed fibromyalgia, and now I have been able to change the medicines; now I take what is natural, and the pain has diminished importantly."

In the cognitive benefits, it has been found that those who practice mindfulness increase their ability to focus and decrease the distractors (Moore & Malinowski, 2009). The interviewees expressed that the benefits are related to higher concentration and attention:

Luis Eugenio mentioned, "I am less distracted; I disagree less. Frequently, I have been working better for myself."

Josefina recognizes, "I have improved my ability to concentrate."

Adriana, on the other hand, mentions, "One of the benefits is to silence the mind.…"

For Jesus. "The benefit is when you are making decisions because you are already present."

Within the emotional benefits, there is evidence that shows that mindfulness helps to develop an effective emotional regulation in the brain (Dunne, 2015).

In this regard, Eduardo mentions: ", that you do not feel that your emotional intelligence affects you ---to feel calm, optimistic and confident to face the challenges of every day."

Alejandra, on the other hand, mentions, "... to make my reactions based on my emotions. I realized that I am an emotional illiterate, I could not name what I felt ... I learned to identify my feelings; for me, that was the best thing."

Karina helps her order her emotions: "give me the opportunity to arrange them as if I were ordering the contents in my drawers."

Edgar mentioned that the pressures of work are powerful, and they can lead executives to problems of depression, alcoholism, or other problems; for him, mindfulness is a tool to counteract them "...let us give him this balm, lubricant or mental and emotional balance because this is a Formula One race and it is truly tense."

Josefina mentioned that it has helped her with depression due to fibromyalgia: "... depression, I see it as the loss of consciousness...Mindfulness is a tool that helps me find meaning in what I do and with it, I reduce my depression."

For Adriana, Mindfulness has helped her to stay positive. "Yes, I remain for a longer time with a positive attitude, positive thoughts. A mood of progress, of being active, rather than having feelings of defeat."

Regarding the spiritual benefits, only two interviewees mentioned this theme:

"...To be aligned with your body, your mind, and your spirit to one thing."

Benefits Generated in the Organization

The perceived benefits for the organization from the interviewees are related to the idea that organizations are made up of people, and that when they are better, then the organization benefits. This idea is mentioned by Jesus "mindfulness is not for work. It is for you as a person, and when you are in a state of well-being, where you can feel full and happy, you will work better and more effectively."

To facilitate the understanding of the benefits generated by mindfulness in the organization the analysis took the five factors founded by Baer et al. (2006) when evaluating how collaborators reported the benefits of this practice. These factors are:

1. *Observing* includes noting internal and external experiences such as sensations, cognitions, emotions, images, sounds, and smells. "Includes being able to see both, the big and the small picture" (Reina, 2022, p. 62).
2. *Describing* refers to labeling intimate experiences with words. "...acknowledge the presence of something, give it a name, and then let it go" (Reina, 2022, p. 59).
3. *Acting with awareness* refers to carrying out activities with attention and not with an automatic pilot. "Being on autopilot are the opposite of mindfulness, then mindfulness should be understood as a take of being conscious, awake, aware" (Mortlock, 2022, p. 261).
4. *Nonjudging* is to take a non-evaluative posture regarding feelings and thoughts. "Mindful individuals are aware that they thoughts and emotions are exactly that. Thoughts are simply the cognitions that occur in the head, and emotions are the reactions to these cognitions" (Reina, 2022, p. 61).
5. *Nonreactivity* is allowing thoughts and feelings to come and go without being trapped or carried away by them. "Individuals who experience nonreactivity are fully engaged in the world but do not get derailed when a negative event happens" (Reina, 2022, p. 60).

Observing

At this point, 10 of the 12 responders noted that their ability to observe improved;

Edgar mentioned, "... the mindfulness tool connects you...you are living it, you consent to the experience, and you say: this is what life is about ... you are not the thoughts that come to your mind."

Jesus commented; "... you can remove the cobwebs that you wear on your head; it helps you to have your senses aligned to what you are. It gives you a grater observation, a greater feeling."

Alejandra mentioned, "In other words, what are the emotions that you are going through. It is not only fear, it is anguish, it is the feeling of sadness, for me that little picture was a great revelation."

Regarding external experiences, the most identified by the interviewees are related to the valuing of what surrounds them, appreciating the views, the small details of daily life. For example:

> Luis Eugenio commented: "I would almost say a lot of that at the beginning. It was very evident when I would go out for walks in the morning doing my exercising, I would begin to realize that the air was blowing; that there were smells."

> Meanwhile, Edgar would say, "... you smell the coffee, you feel the aroma. I see how warm it is, you check the fine foam that was created right now as you added the milk... all those kind of things. You fly and you become conscious and you enjoy daily life much more."

> Guadlupe mentioned, "It's as if the sensations were more intense."

> Karina commented, "Many things have changed in my life, but I'm more alert because I'm not worried anymore; I feel like I see my surroundings more."

Describing

When trying to describe their experiences, eleven of the twelve interviewees mentioned that they did recognize their feelings in a better way, although not everyone was capable of verbalizing them. For example:

> Edgar said, "you note when you are on the verge of bursting; you take a break. Mindfulness as a first stage makes you more aware of yourself."

> Karina: "I am not going to tell you that I express it more, but yes I become more aware."

> Adriana: "Suddenly one says that in this mood in which I find myself there is more sadness or joy. Yes, I can recognize it better."

> Jesus mentions: "It helps to recognize what you feel, and the sensations or feelings expressed in body, such as temperature, heat, in certain areas of the body, you are noticing it. As the body is reacting to the feeling and you identify it."

Adris comments: "It has helped me because sometimes situations or emotions may have happened to which you did not give a name... since simply having a name for you is much easier to identify and work based on that, and I think that mindfulness helps a lot."

On the other hand, there were those who acknowledged that it also helps him to communicate in a better way as Luis Eugenio says: "...you feel as if things that used to be a flood, now you can talk and communicate more leisurely."

Acting with Awareness

All the interviewees recognized that mindfulness helped them not to do several things at once, but to prioritize and consciously make them one at a time, making them more efficient and productive. For example:

Luis Eugenio commented: "Review your 17 things. It is urgent to do 5 and 9. Then the only thing I have noticed is that I put myself in 5."

Eduardo recognizes that: "I think it is an indirect benefit ... focus and concentration."

Alejandra commented: "For the fact of not being worried in all the slopes and saying good because this day I will dedicate it to research ... nothing more ... the world can turn, but I am in one thing."

Karina acknowledged: "Previously I could not concentrate on what I was doing because I was in 25 things... zero concentration ... now, this is the opposite."

Adriana mentions that it helps her to respond: "Previously, I was more reactive. before I was more reactive. I have learned to be more silent with my comments."

Nonjudging

Mindfulness contributed with everyone to come aware of the judgment about others, as well as the judgments made about themselves. For example:

Luis Eugenio expresses: "Mindfulness helped me see other faces ... the person cannot be as I want it to be, then give him his chance .. with me it is the same."

Eduardo comments: "The reality is that if I was a little or a lot, critical, so to speak, and sometimes makes superficial judgments without having the information, mindfulness helped me to give myself a little more maturity to be careful in not making value judgements ... this was an indisputable benefit."

Guadalupe recognizes that "It is great to be aware of interpretations because how that simplifies life, so good."

On the other hand, Adris recognizes that the main benefit is to diminish the way she nudges herself: "I always self-judge a lot that... you cannot be sad, you cannot get angry, you have to follow, and I realized that there are times when you can be sad or maybe you do not want to talk to anyone and it´s okay."

Nonreactivity

All the interviewees recognize that the practice of mindfulness has helped them to let go of the thoughts that cause them anxiety, anguish, and stress. For example:

Eduardo: "It is out of my hands, so do not worry about it ... That is what I think has been a positive change, the same effect of blocking those anxieties and stress in a structured way, with this program, it helps you start the clean day."

Alejandro comments: "It helped me a lot because part of those catastrophic thoughts and telenovela (soap opera) is because you are futurizing and mindfulness is anchored in today, right now."

Josefina: "I can get rid of them easier, do not do soap operas and that if I have it very clear, that any negative thing that occurs to me, before I get all the soap opera I already did it aside."

Karina sees it as a tool that helps her to be at peace. "Calm down, breathe, why is it happening? What can you do? To have the tools and be there in peace, not with past but with what is."

In the case of Adriana, she acknowledged that it helped her out more quickly from sadness left by the death of a friend. "I admit to myself that I would have stayed in a depressed state of sadness for a much longer time."

Anais recognized that in the past, everything was anguish, "... and now I realize and I wonder, but what could I do? Well, I cannot do anything and I lose it, and continue, because if I did not, it would ruin me all day."

In all the factors, explicit and tangible benefits are recognized with the practice of mindfulness. This is important to mention since it does not matter how one gets to practice; that is, if you come because you are interested in looking for tools that help you with your day to day, or you get skeptical and without knowing anything about it.

DISCUSSION ABOUT THE BENEFITS OF MINDFULNESS AT WORK AND COLLABORATORS

The results show that while mindfulness programs at work benefit employees, it is the organizations that take the most significant benefit by having more committed, more productive, more efficient employees with less stress. In this way, mindfulness programs are offered both individually and organizationally, impacting the five factors previously identified by the literature, and produce mainly physical, cognitive, and emotional benefits.

Speaking of the benefits that the organization has to offer mindfulness to its collaborators, the following are recognized. Everyone recognizes that the organization benefits from having more balanced, less stressed, and more focused collaborators; however, it was notorious how the collaborators of the two institutions define them in different ways.

Fort he directors of Daltile, they say that the benefits for the organization are that they are more productive, more assertive in decision-making that they improve their leadership style and their relationships with their work team. For example:

Eduardo commented: "Being less time overwhelmed and distressed by problems and being able to focus more time on solutions and keep moving forward. It makes you more productive, without a doubt."

For his part, Edgar recognizes that: "My evolution of my leadership style ... for my leadership is summarized in to things... to align and put in your side minds and hearts of people."

Another manager mentioned: "Yes, helps a lot in negotiations to be more empathetic, better customer service helps you to stay more motivated when suddenly you feel some fatigue, you relax a few minutes, take a moment of breathing, you focus again and you start."

Jesus mentions that his changes are in the 360 evaluation: "One of the opportunities of a few years ago was that I exploited very often, and in the last two years, it is one of my strengths; On the other hand, having managers and executives with better emotional control, more stable, leads you to make assertive decisions and that becomes results."

On the other hand, in the university the professors see that the main benefit for the university is that their teachers are much better with the treatment and the service to the students.

Adris comments: "I am always seeing how to benefit my students with mindfulness..."

Alejandra mentions that now her students are looking for her when they are going through difficult moments, and she can accompany them in their processes: "I have had experiences that my students are going through emotionally difficult moments and that thanks to that I am more open to listening to them and I am more sensitive. I have been able to help them."

For Josefina, the practice of mindfulness helped her to improve her learning activities, besides feeling more committed and grateful to the institution because I know that all this is worth much money and they give it to me just for registering.

Karina is grateful: "I feel that the university was concerned because I was well; it makes me feel calm ... I can be in class and be there. I enjoy it more ..." and Adriana comments that "It is gratifying that thee are institutions that are interested in their collaborators. Now I am more efficient in my classes because I do not get involved additional discussions with my students."

For Guadalupe and Anais, who work at the CID the benefits for the organization reflect in an increase in their commitment to the institution, becoming more productive and working better as a team.

Although in Mexico there is a controversy about the sincere interest of the companies of Mexico offering mindfulness workshops; that is, if the interest for the collaborators is genuine or they do it to benefit in some way in their earnings. What is clear is that this is irrelevant because the benefits that employees receive from learning mindfulness are undeniable and tangible for both the organization and their personal lives.

Once a mindful attitude is integrated into the organization, all of them benefit from its results. Employees increase their levels of well-being, reducing stress, building positive relationships, developing an emotional intelligence that allows them to regulate before any experience, as well as increase in empathy toward others and shared objectives.

Summary

Technological advances generate constant stimuli to be globally hyperlinked with constant distractions. This is causing mental, physical, and emotional epidemics and with them the decrease in productivity and the well-being of people. Mindfulness is a perfect tool to help counteract the aforementioned. The results shown in this chapter provide information that helps human resource managers and leaders in organizations to decide to design wellness programs for their employees where mindfulness is one of the tools offered.

Mindfulness is a practice that develops the ability of the mind to be aware of what happens internally and externally to redirect attention to the present moment and cultivate healthy habits. Being in the present allows us to concentrate on what is important, and therefore the practices of mindfulness recognize the following benefits: a decrease in nominative thoughts, increase in empathy, increase in flexible responses, emotional regulation, and the increase in self-determination.

On the other hand, the organization having more balanced collaborators obtains the following benefits: Reduction of stress and anxiety states. Increased attention and concentration, emotional self-regulation, increased quality in decision-making, increase positive interpersonal relationships, increase in intelligent empathy, increased flexibility, less reactivity, increased capacity to further adequately address challenges and difficulties, positive coping of the processes of change, improvement in global performance, and conscious and positive leadership.

Mortlock (2022) states that mindfulness helps to achieve better physical and mental health and better relationships at home and at work. On the other hand it allows individuals to face difficulties in their lives. The training in mindfulness is beneficial for the organizations when it adapts to its culture and to the understanding of the theory and practice from a deeper perspective of this type of practice. Mindfulness has a beneficial property of the teams, organizations, and the people who constitute them, resulting in a relevant aspect to study, promote, and implemente in a context with high levels of depression or stress, such as the case of Mexico.

REFERENCES

Ashmos, D., & Duchon, D. (2000). Spirituality at work. *Journal of Management Inquiry, 9*(2), 134–145.

Baer, R. A., Smith, G. T., Hopkins, J., Krietemeyer, J., & Toney, L. (2006). Using self-report assessment methods to explore facets of mindfulness. *Assessment, 13*(1), 27–45. https://doi.org/10.1177/1073191105283504

Brown, K. W., Ryan, R. M., & Creswell, J. D. (2007). Mindfulness: Theoretical Foundations and Evidence for its Salutary Effects. *Psychological Inquiry, 18*(4), 211–237.

Cacioppe, R. L. (2017). Integral mindflow: A process of mindfulness-in-flow to enhance individual and organization learning. *The Learning Organization, 24*(6), 408–417.

Cruz, A. (2018, May 21). ¿Depresión laboral? *Reporte Indigo.* https://www.rep orteindigo.com/piensa/depresion-laboral-condiciones-trabajo-mexico-afecta ciones-salud-trabajadores/

Damore, D. R., O'Connor, J. A, & Hammons, D. (2004). Eternal work place change: Chaplains' response. *Work, 23*(1), 19–22. http://www.ncbi.nlm.nih.gov/pubmed/15328459

Dorjee, D. (2010). Kinds and dimensions of mindfulness: Why it is important to distinguish them. *Mindfulness, 1*(3), 152–160. https://doi.org/10.1007/s12671-010-0016-3

Dunne, J. D. (2015). Buddhist styles of mindfulness: A heuristic approach. In B. D. Ostafin, M. D. Robinson, & B. P. Meier (Eds.), *Handbook of mindfulness and self-regulation* (pp. 251–270). Springer.

Forbes. (2017, December 21). Mexicanos, los más estresados del mundo por su trabajo. *Forbes.* https://www.forbes.com.mx/mexicanos-los-mas-estres ados-del-mundo-por-su-trabajo/

Hicks, D. A. (2003). *Religion and the workplace: Pluralism, spirituality, leadership* (1st ed.). Cambridge University Press.

Hülsheger, U. R., Alberts, H. J. E. M., Feinholdt, A., & Lang, J. W. B. (2013). Benefits of mindfulness at work: The role of mindfulness in emotion regulation, emotional exhaustion, and job satisfaction. *Journal of Applied Psychology, 98*(2), 310–325. https://doi.org/10.1037/a0031313

Hyland, T. (2017). McDonaldizing spirituality: Mindfulness, education, and consumerism. *Journal of Transformative Education, 15*(4), 334–356.

Kabat-Zinn, J. (2003). Mindfulness-based stress reduction (MBSR). *Constructivism in the Human Sciences, 8*(2), 73.

Krishnakumar, S., & Neck, C. P. (2002). The "what", "why" and "how" of spirituality in the workplace. *Journal of Managerial Psychology, 17*(3), 153–164. https://doi.org/10.1108/02683940210423060

Kuyken, W., Byford, S., Taylor, R. S., Watkins, E., Holden, E., White, K., Barrett, B., Byng, R., Evans, A., Mullan, E., & Teasdale, J. D. (2008). Mindfulness-based cognitive therapy to prevent relapse in recurrent depression. *Journal of Consulting and Clinical Psychology, 76*(6), 966–978.

Mejía, X. (2018, June 24). Depresión afectó en 2017 a 7 mil empleados; IMSS pagó 12 mdp por inhabilitación. *Excelsior.* https://www.excelsior.com.mx/nacional/depresion-afecto-en-2017-a-7-mil-empleados-imss-pago-12-mdp-por-inhabilitacion/1247637

Moore, A., & Malinowski, P. (2009). Meditation, mindfulness and cognitive flexibility. *Consciousness and Cognition, 18*(1), 176–186.

Mortlock, J. T. (2022). More thah meditation. In S. K. Dhiman (Ed.), *The Routledge companion to mindfulness at work* (pp. 251–265). Routledge.

Ogliastri, E., & Zúñiga, R. (2016). An introduction to mindfulness and sensemaking by highly reliable organizations in Latin America. *Journal of Business Research, 69*(10), 4429–4434.

Pang, D., & Ruch, W. (2019). Fusing character strengths and mindfulness interventions: Benefits for job satisfaction and performance. *Journal of Occupational Health Psychology, 24*(1), 150.

Pérez Santiago, J. A. (2007). Estudio exploratorio sobre el tema de la espiritualidad en el ambiente laboral. *Anales de Psicología, 23*(1), 137–146.

Pinck, A. S., & Sonnentag, S. (2018). Leader mindfulness and employee well-being: The mediating role of transformational leadership. *Mindfulness, 9*(3), 884–896.

Portales, L. (2015). El poder de las palabras de los capellanes. El impacto en los colaboradores de la gestión de la espiritualidad laboral. *Estudios Gerenciales, 31*, 212–222. https://doi.org/10.1016/j.estger.2014.12.004

Portales, L., & Garza-Meza, L. (2016). Medición y dimensionalidad de la espiritualidad en líderes organizacionales mexicanos. *Ciencias Administrativas. Teoría y Praxis, 12*(1), 122–139.

Purser, R. E., & Milillo, J. (2014). Mindfulness Revisited: A Buddhist-Based conceptualization. *Journal of Management Inquiry, 24*(1), 3–24. https://doi.org/10.1177/1056492614532315

Reina, C. S. (2022). A multidimensional conceptualization of minfulness at work. In S. K. Dhiman (Ed.), *The Routledge companion to mindfulness at work* (pp. 54–80). Routledge.

Rodríguez Zárate, C. E. (2018, April 24). Enfrentando el Síndrome Estrés del siglo XXI. *Forbes México.* https://www.forbes.com.mx/enfrentando-el-sindrome-estres-del-siglo-xxi/

Roth, B., & Stanley, T. W. (2002). Mindfulness-based stress reduction and healthcare utilization in the inner city: Preliminary findings. *Alternative Therapies in Health and Medicine, 8*(1), 60–62.

Rupprecht, S., Koole, W., Chaskalson, M., Tamdjidi, C., & West, M. (2018). Running too far ahead ? Towards a broader understanding of mindfulness in organisations. *Current Opinion in Psychology, 28*(October), 32–36. https://doi.org/10.1016/j.copsyc.2018.10.007

Segal, Z. V., Williams, J. M. G., & Teasdale, J. D. (2013). *Mindfulness-based cognitive therapy for depression* (2nd ed.). Guilford Press.

Shapiro, S. L., Carlson, L. E., Astin, J. A., & Freedman, B. (2006). Mechanisms of mindfulness. *Journal of Clinical Psychology, 62*(3), 373–386. https://doi.org/10.1016/j.concog.2008.12.008

Siegel, R. D., Germer, C. K., & Olendzki, A. (2009). Mindfulness: What is it? Where did it come from? In F. Didonna (Ed.), *Clinical handbook of mindfulness* (pp. 17–36). Springer. https://doi.org/10.1007/978-0-387-09593-6

Siegrist, J. (2001). A theory of occupational stress. In J. Dunham (Ed.), *Stress in the workplace: Past, present and future* (pp. 52–66). Whurr Publishers.

Siegrist, J., & Wahrendorf, M. (2016). *Work stress and health in a globalized economy.* Springer.

Slutsky, J., Chin, B., Raye, J., & Creswell, J. D. (2018). Mindfulness training improves employee well-being: A randomized controlled trial. *Journal of Occupational Health Psychology, 24*(1), 139–149.

Sutcliffe, K. M., Vogus, T. J., & Dane, E. (2016). Mindfulness in organizations: A cross-level review. *Annual Review of Organizational Psychology and Organizational Behavior, 3*(April), 55–81. https://doi.org/10.1146/annurev-orgpsych-041015-062531

Tuckey, M. R., Sonnentag, S., & Bryan, J. (2018). Are state mindfulness and state work engagement related during the workday? *Work & Stress, 32*(1), 33–48.

Velázquez, E. C., & Lino, M. (2018, July 22). Depresión: en 2020 será la principal causa de discapacidad en México. *Animal Político.* https://www.animalpolitico.com/2018/07/depresion-2020-discapacidad-mexico/

Walsh, Z. D. (2017). Critical theory and the contemporary discourse on mindfulness. *Journal of the International Association of Buddhist Universities (JIABU)*, 9(2), 103–110.

Williams, J. M. G., & Kabat-Zinn, J. (2011). Introduction mindfulness: Diverse perspectives on its meaning, origins, and multiple applications at the intersection of science and dharma. *Contemporary Buddhism, 12*(1), 1–18. https://doi.org/10.1080/14639947.2011.564811

Zinnbauer, B. J., Pargament, K. I., & Scott, A. B. (1999). The emerging meanings of religiousness and spirituality: Problems and prospects. *Journal of Personality, 67*(6), 889–919.

Zivnuska, S., Kacmar, K. M., Ferguson, M., & Carlson, D. S. (2016). Mindfulness at work: Resource accumulation, well-being, and attitudes. *Career Development International, 21*(2), 106–124.

CHAPTER 4

Pursuit of Meaning in Life and Human Flourishing: A Phenomenological Study

Varinder Kumar

Abstract Though meaning in life is one of the indicators of positive functioning, yet scant attention is given to it in organizational context. Positive leadership attempts to facilitate realization of meaning in life for different people. The present chapter attempts to discuss different themes and obstacles in meaning in life after undertaking phenomenology study of different leaders from different fields. The study finds different themes of meaning in life like *ananda* or bliss, happiness and peace of mind, sense of direction, and responsibility for others' well-being. The obstacles to meaning in life include greed, selfish behavior, worldly passions, and confinement to lower order needs. The leaders should overcome these obstacles and realize meaning in life for their spiritual unfolding as well as betterment of the organization.

Keywords Workplace well-being · Meaning in life · Happiness · Ananda

V. Kumar (✉)
Government College of Education, Jalandhar, Punjab, India

© The Author(s), under exclusive license to Springer Nature
Switzerland AG 2023
S. Dhiman (ed.), *New Horizons in Workplace Well-Being*,
https://doi.org/10.1007/978-3-031-17241-0_4

57

INTRODUCTION

Though researchers have included meaning in life as one of the indicators of positive functioning (Diener & Seligman, 2002) or reaching one's potentials (Ryan & Deci, 2001), yet scant attention has been paid to this theme in organizational context. Transformational leaders (Burns, 1978) and its variants like authentic leaders (George, 2003; George & Sims, 2007), ethical leaders (Brown & Trevino, 2006), servant leaders (Greenleaf, 1977), etc., practicing spiritual and ethical values actively search the meaning in their lives and facilitate others to realize meaning of life by providing environment for spiritual growth. They reduce organizational dysfunction and stress impacting organizational performance that lead to meaninglessness (Kumar & Dhiman, 2020; Mitroff & Denton, 1999) and help others to find meanings that ultimately contribute to human flourishing at workplace.

The present paper attempts to explore the contents of meaning in life and its perceived benefits in context of organization by undertaking phenomenology study related with spiritual values that include meaning in life. For this, eight leaders from different fields were interviewed and their responses were analyzed. These respondents include Prof. S. K. Chakravorty, retired professor of IIM-Calcutta; Swami Parmarthananda, Chennai-based Vedanta preacher; Dr. Sakit Sen, Director, Sri Aurobindo Foundation of Integral Management; Laxmi Niwas Junjanwala, well-known business leader; Dr. B. M. Bhardwaj, social worker of Apna Ghar, Bharatpur; Mathieu Ricard, Buddhist monk and social worker; Ms. Santosh Yadav, First lady to climb Mt. Everest *twice* and Dr. E. Sreedharan, popularly known as Metro Man. After tape recording their responses, transcripts were analyzed. These responses were analyzed and studied by three independent interraters. After establishing interrater reliability ≥ 0.67, different themes were identified and elaborated with their direct quotes and statements.

MEANING OF MEANING IN LIFE

Meaning in life entails different personal experiences and their interpretations with transformed attitude. It includes not only life-altering experiences but also understanding the importance beyond "the trivial or momentary [experiences of daily life] to have purpose, or to have coherence that transcend chaos" (King et al., 2006, p. 180). Steger (2012) calls it web of connections, understandings, and interpretations that help us comprehend our experience and formulate plans directing our energies to the achievement of our desired future, as our lives matter, make sense, and are more than days and years. Meaning in life refers to an individual's ability to understand life, oneself, and the outside world and adapt to it accordingly. The Japanese concept, synonym of Meaning in Life, *Ikigai* (Garcia & Miralles, 2016) means "the happiness of always being busy" (p. 2), "keep doing what is being loved for as long as the health allows" (p. 10), and "finding a purpose in life" (p. 14). It involves keeping a Stoic attitude with equanimity despite suffering setbacks and working in high spirit with focused sense of direction. It encompasses both presence as well as search for meaning (Steger, 2012). *Presence of meaning* indicates whether the individual perceives one's life as significant and purposeful, and comprehends oneself as fitted in the surrounding work (King et al., 2006; Steger et al., 2008). *Search for meaning* indicates the strength, intensity, and activity of people to enhance and establish their understanding and purpose of their lives (Steger et al., 2008).

Meaning in life also includes three components: purpose, significance, and coherence (Martela & Steger, 2016; Ward & King, 2017). *Purpose* in life means having a sense of direction, mission, and goal in life; *significance* denotes feeling in an individual that his or her role is being valued in social surrounding and consequently s/he has to make important contribution beyond his or her personal existence; and *coherence* is feeling of order between oneself and the world, and perceiving one's world as comprehensible, manageable, and meaningful.

MEANING IN LIFE-ORGANIZATIONAL STUDIES

In the context of organization and leadership studies, meaning in life. has not been studied except indirect evidences of its benefits for the organization (Ward & King, 2017) and Maslow's indication of spiritual growth at the highest level of hierarchy of human needs manifested in contributing to the well-being of others. Attaining happiness involves realizing the meaning of life along with becoming a holistic person. As meaning in life is associated with spirituality-transcendence, connectedness with higher purpose, and sacredness (Mitroff & Denton, 1999), transformational leaders being fully evolved persons with deep-rooted ethical and spiritual values (Fry, 2003) actively search the meaning of their lives, facilitate in realizing meaning by others, and create work environment supportive of one's spiritual development along with organizational mission. Through their idealized influence and intellectual stimulation, they overcome meaninglessness manifested in the form of organizational dysfunction, ineffectiveness, and stress impacting organizational performance. They also help others to find meaning and happiness at workplace with greater commitment and motivation by making the work more meaningful.

Persons high in meaning in life enjoy their work more and report to lesser workaholism (Bonebright et al., 2000). As meaning in life is positively associated with psychological well-being (Steger et al., 2008), it is also perceived as linked with meaning in work that contributes to engagement, greater organizational commitment and job satisfaction (Geldenhuys et al., 2014; May et al., 2004). Meaningful work is also negatively associated with depressive symptoms, hostility, burnouts, absenteeism, and other negative outcomes at workplace and life (Steger et al., 2012). Many people look to their career as source of meaning as greater amount of time is being spent at workplace these days, and work is perceived as source of understanding world, opportunity to serve others, means to self-expression of one's full potentials, and contributor to attain personal growth and elevation. Transformational leaders not only overcome meaninglessness as manifested in apathy, alienation, frustration, and increased stress (Debats et al., 1995), but also create a work environment that is supportive of increased individual and organizational performance with reduced negativity.

As eudemonic approach emphasizes transcending personal feelings of pleasures to personal elevation and virtuous pursuits (Ryff & Singer, 2003), meaning in life is typically included as one of the important aspects of happiness and well-being. Meaning in life has great motivational power as it inspires and energizes people, gives them hope and optimism especially in adversity, and helps to maintain physical and psychological health. Victor Frankl's work *Man's Search for Meaning* (1959) being elaboration of Nietzsche's quote "He who has a *why* to live can bear with almost any *how*" with authenticity of his experiences as well as stories of his patients related with Nazi concentration camp demonstrates that though human beings cannot avoid suffering yet they can choose to cope with it in a better and effective way by finding meaning in it and move forward with enlightened purpose with spiritual freedom. Meaning in life enables to develop resilience and cultivate a spiritual connectedness with something larger than the momentary experiences (Steger, 2012). Research studies illuminate that meaning in life contributes to psychological and physical health as it is linked with positive emotions (King et al, 2006; Steger et al., 2006), satisfaction in life (Steger et al., 2006), positive perception of the world, and hope and optimism (Mascaro & Rosen 2006; Steger et al., 2006). It is negatively associated with factors depriving happiness: depression (Debats, 1996), anxiety, general psychological distress, and post-traumatic stress disorder (Mascaro & Rosen, 2005). People with meaning in their lives can effectively cope with cancer, spinal cord injuries, cardiovascular diseases, etc. (Steger, 2012). Therefore researchers have included meaning in life as one of the indicators of human flourishing or positive functioning (Diener & Seligman, 2002) or reaching one's potentials (Ryan & Deci, 2001).

RESPONSES OF PHENOMENOLOGY STUDY

A phenomenology study was conducted by asking different respondents about the role of meaning in their personal and professional lives, along with the challenges they have faced and the suggestions they will give to leaders during data collection process related with role of spiritual values in context of transformational leadership. Out of 8 respondents 7 respondents commented on value meaning in life, though the left out respondent Laxmi Niwas Jhunjhunwala (2015) commented in indirect way that at ripe age of near 90 years, "he is concerned with other life" by devoting time to reading spiritual texts. Dr. Sreedharan advocated knowing the spiritual truths and working for the welfare of others for spiritual unfoldment as meaning in life that is reflected from his statement:

> To find meaning in one's life, one should know the spiritual truth. One should know that one has responsibility for the welfare of others. Working for the welfare and well-being of others leads one to know one's meaning of life. However the obstacles in searching the meaning of life are worldly passion, desires and selfishness. To search meaning in life, one should do the things with spiritual attitude. One should cultivate purity of mind and purity of heart. There is one plate in my office: "*Karyam Karomi, Na cha Kinchit, aham Karomi*-Whatever is to be done I do, But in reality I do not do anything."

Like Dr. E. Sreedharan, Dr. Bhardwaj (2016) considers the service of the most vulnerable persons as offerings to God for finding meaning in life, as is evident from his following significant statement:

> In Prabhujis (inmates) we are encountering God. They are God in human form taking our test. Service of these handicapped men can lead one to salvation. Whatever you are doing do it with the spirit that it is offering to God. If they [leaders] do this, they will find meaning in life.

To this perspective, service of other beings is sacred that contributes to meaning in life as advocated in Bhagavad Gita as *lokasangraha* (work done for the sake of the humanity at large-B.G. 3.20, 3.25). Dr. Sen (2014) also indicated it with experiencing vedic wisdom *Amritasya Putra* [means Children of immorality—Rig Veda 1.170.4]—we are portion of divinity "to awaken one's inherent potential and to express through one's work as worship." But for this, one has to look at the larger picture of life targeted at eternal objective of life that leads to liberation:

> What is the larger picture. What is the aim of life. If that larger picture is very much clear then you can set goals and objectives.....If the larger picture is clear what are the present circumstances and situation, these are found momentary because I am part of eternal.

Santosh Yadav also indicates that for economic, mental, and spiritual progress in a harmonious way, one has to know the meaning of life. Therefore to find the meaning of life, "one has to introspect whether one has come for *bhoga* [enjoyment of temporary comforts of life] or to serve the society [to repay eternal debts[1]]." Because limitless desires for materialistic pleasures and success are the hindrance to finding meaning in

---

[1] Hindu scriptures like **Manusamhita** lays down five common debts or mahayanas for all householders (These corroborate with Brihadarnyaka Upanishad):

> *Deva rin*: debts to Godsprathana, samarpan, or prayer and surrender of lowerself.
> *Rishi rin*: debts to the seers of Truth-swadhyaya, abhyasa or self-study of shastras, and practice.
> *Pitri rin*: debts to parents and ancestors-seva, tarpan, shraddh, or service, or offering of water etc. to the ancestors.
> *Nri rin*: debts to humanity at large-danam or charity.
> *Bhuta rin*: debts to sub-human species-sanrakshan or conservation.

life as they result in losing peace of mind (Yadav, 2019), these should be rationalized and reduced to necessary things and objectives. "For peace of mind, leaders should focus on meaning of life as they can attain divinity in life. Everything is possible, if they attempt to attain it."

Taking standpoint of view from Maslow's human hierarchy needs that lead to basic needs to security, to social needs, to esteem needs, and to realization—Swami Parmarthananda says that when superficial needs of life are taken care, mind plays spiritual playing: Why I am?, Where I am?, What I am doing?, etc. However, "meaning [in life] is inbuilt. If it is not there, other challenges are overpowering. If I am hungry, I will not ask what is the meaning of life." Therefore one has to move from basic needs to higher level needs. Transformational leaders create an environment that facilitates moving from basic, security and social needs to higher level of needs. Whereas negative leadership like corporate psychopaths deliberately create an environment that deprive the person opportunities for growth and finding meaning in life by depleting others' time, toil, and talent.[2]

To Mathieu Ricard (2018), "meaning is life provides sense of direction." He told that once Dalai Lama was asked about "What is the meaning of life?" Dalai Lama replied, "I do not know the meaning of life. We should not be so concerned to meaning, but what meaning you can give to your own life" (Ricard, 2018). Meaning in life with clear sense of direction contributes to own flourishing as well as flourishing of others. With that the leaders bring happiness to their lives and lives of others. Therefore Mathieu Ricard advises leaders,

> Try to see within yourself, what are the values that give greater satisfaction where you will not find selfishness, you will not find greed, pride, but you will find inner peace, inner freedom, generosity, compassion, altruistic love, caring for others, being open mind-all these qualities will give you meaning to your life and will act as meaning to others.

From Prof. Chakraborty's perspective, Indian terminology for meaning in life is seeking *Ananda* or Bliss which is quite different from

---

[2] This fact as based upon researcher's experience in context of educations institutions has been stated in researcher's paper: Kumar, V., & Modi, S. (2022). Leading in new VUCA environment: Role of positive leadership through spiritual and ethical values. In S. Dhiman & J. Marques (Eds.), *Leadership after COVID-19*. Future of Business and Finance. Springer. https://doi.org/10.1007/978-3-030-84867-5_31.

sukha (pleasures) and "Indian psychology can be given another name Anadaology." This Ananda/bliss is possible with simple and contended life as different Indian saints have skipped Maslow's hierarchy of needs to reach higher stage of self-realization, even higher than the Western concept of self-actualization. In Indian culture, the appropriate word for meaning in life is "delight or joy in life" (Chakraborty, 2014) and Taittiriya Upanishad with Ananda Valli section is dedicated to Ananda. This Ananda comes with self-realization and otherism motivation as Prof. Chakraborty states, "Whosoever carries otherish motivation, attends to others' problem, with keeping oneself in background will find ananda. On the other hand, the person with self-centredness will find vacuum in life." Therefore he gives advice to others, "stop running after rank order, ananda will be spontaneous. Whatsoever varana you belong, treat work as door to Moksha. Moksha is the ultimate goal of life."

After discussion of the value related with meaning in life, the common themes emerging are Ananda/bliss, happiness and peace of mind, sense of direction, and responsibility for others' well-being. However the common obstacles in realizing meaning in life are selfishness and greed, lack of direction, worldly passions, and confinement to lower order needs.

COMMON THEMES OF MEANING IN LIFE

Different common themes identified from the above discussion are:

- Ananda/bliss (Chakraborty, 2014; Swami Parmarthananda, 2014)
- Happiness and peace of mind (Ricard, 2018; Yadav, 2019)
- Sense of direction (Ricard, 2018; Sen, 2014)
- Responsibility for others' well-being (Bhardwaj, 2016; Sreedharan, 2019)

Ananda or Bliss

Prof. S. K. Chakraborty (2014) and Swami Parmarthananda (2014) indicate meaning in life with attaining the ecstatic state of Ananda or Bliss. This Ananda is a state of trance or Samadhi when the mind becomes free from modifications and one remains contented in the Self alone (B.G. 6.20). This state is beyond five senses (B.G. 6.21) and is attained when one does not think of any other acquisition to be superior to that (6.22) and lives in silence and stillness with the practice of Yoga by transcending five senses, mind, and intellect. Anadavali section of Taittririya Upanishad talks about different layers or sheaths in which consciousness is enveloped. Accordingly, ultimate bliss—Ananda is hidden in the inner layer within superficial layers of existence, and is the abode of peace, bliss, and tranquility. After attaining this state, one becomes one with all reality with no separation between object and subject.

Happiness and Peace of Mind

Meaning in life is the source of ultimate happiness and peace of mind (Ricard, 2018; Yadav, 2019). Happiness is "deep sense of flourishing that arises from an exceptionally healthy mind-an optimum state of being" (Ricard, 2008, p. 19). For this state of happiness, not only successful economic pursuits, feeling of emotional satisfaction with surrounding people, but finding meaning in work and life contribute a lot. Unlike materialistic pursuits and pleasures that are momentary, sensual, and dependent upon external circumstances, happiness is an everlasting state of mind—human flourishing, which is not dependent upon external circumstances. As one becomes dependent upon external circumstances, situation, or persons, one becomes miserable. Therefore Manu Samriti defines happiness in terms of attaining state of non-dependence upon external objects, persons, and situations. दुःखं सर्वमात्मवशं सुखं, एतत् विधात समासेन लक्षणं सुख दुःखयोः (Liberty—in all respects, is happiness and dependence—in all matters is misery. Know these to be the general definitions of happiness and misery—Manu Smriti, IV. 160) (Swami Parmarthananda, 2003, p. 2). As one realizes this state of non-dependence upon external circumstances, one feels happiness and meaning in one's life.

Sense of Direction

Mathieu Ricard (2018) identifies sense of direction contributing to meaning in Life. Western psychologists talk about focus (Goleman, 2013) and flow (Csikszentmihalyi, 1990) for bringing direction in life that contributes to meaning in life. For leaders, Goleman (2013) talks about cultivating three kinds of focus: inner focus attuned to intuitions and values, other focus smoothing connection with people around oneself and focus on larger system. A person or leader "tuned out of his internal world will be rudderless; one blind to the world of others will be clueless; those indifferent to the larger systems within which they operate will be blindsided" (Goleman, 2013, p. 4). For cultivating focus, one needs to cultivate profound attention which works much like a muscle becoming stronger with greater use. Therefore for attaining meaning in life, one has to cultivate focus with meditative thinking and work on that persistently. Similarly to attain flow in different moments, one feels involved and works in effortless efforts with greater level of clarity of goals, commitment, competence or skills, concentration, and challenges. Autolelic individuals, more guided by their inner compass, have strong sense of purpose and are more likely to experience flow in life and consequently experience meaning in life.

Responsibility for Others' Well-Being

Dr. E. Sreedharan (2019) identifies responsibility for others' well-being as one of the themes of meaning in life. The persons aspiring for meaning in life feel responsibility and inner calling for their contribution to the happiness of their organization, their people, society, family, nation, globe, and environment. To Dr. E. Sreedharan (2017), "completion of the projects on time without cost overruns is not only question of professional competence, but of social responsibility as these projects are pursued with people's money." This concept of social responsibility involves sensitivity and mindfulness of the leaders that virtually extends to universal responsibility of conserving the environment in light of depleting resources and working on principles of sustainability, contributing to the peace of the planet, contributing to the happiness of people with positive human qualities such as tolerance and love. Responsibility for others' well-being also involves taking care of weaker sections of the globe, transforming the lives of people with positive influence, and ensuring freedom of everyone by treating them decently with respect and dignity. As one gives and contributes to the happiness and well-being of others, one finds meaning in life. Therefore Dalai Lama (quoted in Ricard, 2013) advocates to pursue universal responsibility with elimination of petty self-interests and by viewing altruistic action as an opportunity to serve for other's happiness and to eradicate their sufferings:

To acquire a sense of universal responsibility-to perceive the universal dimension of each of our actions and each person's duty towards happiness and non-suffering-is to acquire a state of mind that, when we see an opportunity to help others, drives us to seize it rather than worrying solely about our own petty self-interest. (p. 683)

Vedānta talks of *Nishkam karma*—doing actions without being attached to results or sense of doership, and treating work or actions as offering to the Divine. This selfless service can be offered in numerous ways like financial assistance, physical help, emotional and spiritual support, etc. The aim of selfless service is to contribute to the welfare and well-being of others through thoughts, words, and actions without expectations of reward. Mahatma Gandhi—rare example of transformational, ethical, and servant leadership who devoted his life for the freedom and upliftment of his countrymen-remarked profoundly, "The best way to find yourself is to lose yourself in the service of others."

Obstacles in Realizing Meaning in Life

As per discussion of different leaders, different obstacles in realizing meaning in life include:

- Greed (Yadav, 2019)
- Worldly passions (Sreedharan, 2019)
- Selfishness (Chakraborty, 2014; Ricard, 2018)
- Confinement to lower order needs (Swami Parmarthananda, 2014)

Greed

As per the description of Santosh Yadav (2019), greed for power and materialistic pursuit acts as a barrier to meaning in life. The concept of greed is primarily an excessive desire related with materialistic needs (Balot, 2001, p. 1) or material wealth (American Heritage Dictionary, 2011). The Greek synonym for the word greed is *pleonexia* that means "the desire to acquire more of something (whether that object is tangible, wealth, or intangible, honor or power) in a manner that either takes that good from another, or prohibits another from accessing or acquiring that good" (Burghart, 2015, p. 8). Different themes that touch the definition of greed include selfishness, acquisitive motivation, immorality

(Robertson, 2001, p. 5), injustice and exploitation because of lack of distributive fairness (Balot, 2001, pp. 80–82). To Long (2008, 2009) the four elements of greed include individualism and selfishness, ignoring and avoiding signs of greed-ridden environment, presence of compliances justifying the greedy behavior, and treating others as instruments to be used and discarded. The underlying characteristics of manifested greed are selfishness directed at acquisition of power and possessions, violation of moral norms, creation of environment fostering greed, and exploitation and injustice. Such negative behaviors are likely to affect the happiness and well-being of oneself as well as others. It ultimately deprives one of the meaning in life.

Worldly Passions

Like Santosh Yadav, Dr. E. Sreedharan (2019) identifies too much pursuit of worldly passions as a barrier to meaning in life. Gross ignorance and illusion that worldly passions like materialistic possessions, power, and pursuit of pleasures contribute to happiness is the cause of human sufferings and miseries. Their senseless pursuit causes dependence upon them due to attachment with them. But the feeling of power, control, and pleasure are a temporary and transitory phenomenon. However as the person develops attachment with objects, situations, and persons, s/he becomes dependent upon them which ultimately leads to sorrow (Swami Parmarthananda, 2003, pp. 1–3).

In Indian philosophy, ignorance of the self or lack of self-knowledge is the root cause of all sufferings. Because of nescient ignorance, we value unreal as Real and develop undue attachment to the objects and persons we desire, which becomes the cause of anxiety, stress, and restlessness and ultimately leads toward sufferings and deprives one of the meaning in life.

To cultivate happiness, one should learn to discriminate between what is transient and what is eternal, and develop profound sense of calm and equanimity which is possible through discriminative analysis and dispassion toward illusive world of ever changing emotions and other temporary phenomenon of the phenomenal world. *Viveka*—discrimination between transient and eternal, and *viragya*—detachment toward the illusive world and negating the illusory superimpositions are the time-tested *Vedantic* Wisdom for cultivating profound focus on the real Self, creating conditions of everlasting happiness within and around oneself, and serving the world as liberated being—free from physical, mental, and intellectual entanglements.

As man interacts in the world, s/he develops one or other type of attachment, which becomes bondage. As a result, s/he suffers because of attachment with persons, materialistic objects, and body-mind mechanism. Attachment may provide some psychological satisfaction but it anaesthetizes our sensitivity and impairs our judgment. As we develop attachment with external objects and persons to satisfy our vasanas (inner inclinations) or to accommodate changing moods, we destroy the equipoise which Sankara calls as "dire death" (maha mritu). Thus attachment is short-term gains and long-term pains. S/he who controls her or his own delusory misconceptions (moha) and is not tempted by the external world, finds ultimate solace and contemplation because of liberation from entanglements (Vivekacudamani, Shaloka 85). Shaloka 2.62 and 2.63 of Bhagavad Gita link attachment with downfall and destruction of human being.

Selfish Behavior

Prof. Chakraborty (2014) states selfish behavior as a barrier to realizing meaning in life. Selfish behavior is pursued either with or without considering the interests of others and implications of one's act upon others. Selfish motivation means "simply to benefit oneself without considering the implications of their actions for the well-beings of others" (Crocker et al., 2017, p. 301). In selfish behavior, there is lack of empathic concern for others. People's primarily self-centered, self-interested, and selfish behavior is manifested in narcissism with greater entitlements and exploitative tendencies, behaving without ethics and empathy, aspiration for fame and fortune in quick way, pursuit of hidden agenda because of jealousy with others, short cuts and compromises with ethics and values, egoistic care, tendencies to manage others' impression about oneself, unmitigated communion, i.e., giving others with expectation of reward in future, vindictiveness and arbitrary interpretation and enforcement of rules at the altar of organizational objectives and human values, manipulating others and diverting others' attention on useless and unnecessary matters, opportunism, nepotism, concealing and deliberate misinterpretation of information, showmanship, etc.

Though selfish behavior helps to gain obvious benefits like greater resources, power, and pleasure in short run, yet it involves certain associated costs like highly correlated with poor psychological well-being, physical health and relationship (Kasser et al., 2014), smoking and drinking (Dittmar et al., 2014), negative self-appraisals (self-doubt, self-discrepancy, and self ambivalence), feeling of guilt and regret in the long run, lower-life satisfaction and higher envy (Krekels & Pandelaere, 2015), increased anxiety and depression over time (Crocker et al., 2010), emotional confusion (Canevello & Crocker, 2015), greater loneliness (Crocker & Canevello, 2008), social anxiety due to pursuit of impression management goals, psychological distress due to expectations from others (Fritz & Helgeson, 1998), worse cardiovascular diseases (Cheng et al., 2013), and deteriorated relations with others. Ultimately, selfish behavior causes unhappiness and consequently deprives one to realize meaning in life. As a result, the person finds life empty and void.

Confinement to Lower Order Needs

Swami Parmarthananda (2014) identifies confinement to lower order needs that Maslow talks, one of the obstacles in realizing meaning in life. Maslow (1943) proposed five stage model of human hierarchy needs that ascends from physical needs, to safety needs, to love and belonging, to esteem needs, and to self-actualization at the highest level. His later model was expanded to include cognitive, aesthetic, and transcendence needs (Maslow, 1970). To him, happy persons would have fulfilled these eight levels of needs ranging from concrete to abstract, down to earth to divine needs. The top of these two abstract needs—self-actualization signifies realizing one's personal meaning in life and transcendence means becoming an integrated person and being a valuable part of the world. As one remains confined to lower order needs like struggle in economic, safety, and social needs, one is deprived of ascending to the next level on the ladder of human hierarchy. However there are saints, sages, and realized beings who despite living in poverty skipped this level of need and gave meaning to their lives with spiritual elevation and by serving the society. As they transcended economic, emotional, and existential bottlenecks in their eternal pursuit, they found meaning. But the person caught in economic grind, emotional bickering, or existential crisis fails to realize meaning in life unless s/he perceives it as special design of the Existence to elevate him or her to next level of consciousness.

MEANING IN LIFE: LESSONS FOR LEADERS

Pursuit of meaning in life by leaders contributes to spiritual unfolding and self-realization that adds to human flourishing of oneself and other beings. Leaders high in meaning in life enjoy their work and also contribute to happiness of others. As leadership is extension of oneself, pursuit of meaning in life enables the leader to emit positive emotions along with thieving at work that ultimately contributes to the well-being and human flourishing of others. Transformational leaders with their idealized influence and individualized consideration create conducive environment that supports other staff members to realize meaning in life.

The main obstacles in realizing meaning in life are selfishness, greed for power and possession, indulgence in worldly passions, and pursuits or confinement to lower order needs. Leaders should avoid selfish behavior and greed for power and possession. They should consider it their duty to serve others than to exert power in meaningless ways. To enable others to attain their higher order of needs, they should inspire others with their living examples and create such environment as satisfies the basic needs along with aspiration for realizing meaning in life. As too much indulgence in materialistic possessions and pleasures, deprives one to realize meaning in life, one should try to minimize one's needs with focus on essentials and elimination of inessentials (Yadav, 2019).

Most of the problems in individual and organizational life are due to self-ignorance and taking perspective from body-mind mechanism as it leads to egoistic behavior. As leaders become self-aware to experience Ananda or bliss, they come to know that other beings are manifestation of the Universal consciousness and consequently should not be treated as raw material for magnificence of ego. They should be cared, not coerced. This realization will prevent exploitation, greed, harassment and other abuses. As they consider their power and position as opportunity to serve others with cultivation of profound focus and right direction, they realize meaning in life that is fruitful for their spiritual unfolding as well as betterment of the organization.

References

American Heritage Dictionary. (2011). *American Heritage Dictionary of the English language*. Houghton Miffin.

Balot, R. K. (2001). *Greed and injustice in classical Athens*. Princeton University Press.

Bhardwaj, B. M. (2016). *Personal communication with author* (An Unpublished Source).

Bonebright, C. A., Clay, D. L., & Ankenmann, R. D.(2000). The relationship of workaholism with work–life conflict, life satisfaction, and purpose in life. *Journal of Counseling Psychology, 47*(4), 469–477

Brown, M. E., & Trevino, L. K. (2006). Ethical leadership: A review and future directions. *The Leadership Quarterly, 17*, 595–616.

Burghart, W. D. (2015). *How things fall apart: Pleonexia, parasitic greed and decline in Greek thought from Thucydides to Polybius* (Ph.D. Dissertation). Graduate School of University of Maryland.

Burns, J. (1978). *Leadership*. Harper & Row.

Canevello, A., & Crocker, J. (2015). How self-image and compassionate goals shape intrapsychic experiences. *Social and Personality Psychology Compass, 9*, 620–629.

Chakraborty, S. K. (2014). *Personal communication with author* (An Unpublished Source).

Cheng, J. T., Tracy, J. L., & Miller, G. E. (2013). Are narcissists hardy or vulnerable? The role of narcissism in the production of stress-related biomarkers in response to emotional distress. *Emotion, 13*(6), 1004–1011. https://doi.org/10.1037/a0034410

Crocker, J., & Canevello, A. (2008). Creating and undermining social support in communal relationships: The role of compassionate and self-image goals. *Journal of Personality and Social Psychology, 95*(3), 555–575. https://doi.org/10.1037/0022-3514.95.3.555

Crocker, J., Canevello, A., Breines, J. G., & Flynn, H. (2010). Interpersonal goals and change in anxiety and dysphoria in first-semester college students. *Journal of Personality and Social Psychology, 98*(6), 1009–1024. https://doi.org/10.1037/a0019400

Crocker, J., Canevello, A., & Brown, A. A. (2017). Social motivation: Costs and benefits of selfishness and otherishness. *Annual Review of Psychology, 68*, 299–325.

Csikszentmihalyi, M. (1990). *Flow: The psychology of optimal experience*. Harper and Row.

Debats, D. L., Drost, J., & Hansen, P. (1995). Experiences of meaning in life: A combined qualitative and quantitative approach. *British Journal of Psychology, 86*, 359–375.

Debats, D. L. (1996). Meaning in life: Clinical relevance and predictive power. *British Journal of Clinical Psychology, 35*, 503–516.

Diener, E., & Seligman, M. E. P. (2002). Very happy people. *Psychological Science, 13*(1), 81–84.

Dittmar, H., Bond, R., Hurst, M., & Kasser, T. (2014). The relationship between materialism and personal well-being: A meta-analysis. *Journal of Personality and Social Psychology, 107*(5), 879–924. https://doi.org/10.1037/a0037409

Frankl, V. E. (1959). *Man's search for meaning: An introduction to logotherapy.* Random House.

Fritz, H. L., & Helgeson, V. S. (1998). Distinctions of unmitigated communion from communion: Self-neglect and overinvolvement with others. *Journal of Personality and Social Psychology, 75*(1), 121–140.

Fry, L. W. (2003). Toward a theory of spiritual leadership. *The Leadership Quarterly, 14*, 693–727.

Garcia, R., & Miralles, F. (2016). *Ikigai: The Japanese secret to a long and happy life.* Hutchinson.

Geldenhuys, M., Laba, K., & Venter, C. M. (2014). Meaningful work, work engagement and organisational commitment. *SA Journal of Industrial Psychology, 40*(1), 1–10.

George, B. (2003). *Authentic leadership.* Jossey-Bass.

George, B., & Sims, P. (2007). *True north: Discover your authentic leadership.* Jossey Bass.

Goleman, D. (2013). *Focus: The hidden driver to excellence.* Bloomsbury.

Greenleaf, R. K. (1977). *Servant leadership.* Paulist Press.

Jhunjhunwala, L. N. (2015). *Personal communication with author* (An Unpublished Source).

Kasser, T., Rosenblum, K. L., Sameroff, A. J., Deci, E. L., Niemiec, C. P., et al. (2014). Changes in materialism, changes in psychological well-being: Evidence from three longitudinal studies and an intervention experiment. *Motivation and Emotion, 38*, 1–22.

King, L. A., Hicks, J., Krull, J., & Del Gaiso, A. K. (2006). Positive affect and the experience of meaning in life. *Journal of Personality and Social Psychology, 90*(1), 179–196.

Krekels, G., & Pandelaere, M. (2015). Dispositional greed. *Personality and Individual Differences, 74*, 225–230. https://doi.org/10.1016/j.paid.2014.10.036

Kumar, V., & Dhiman, S. (2020). Happiness and workplace well-being: Transformational leadership and the role of ethical and spiritual values. In *The Palgrave handbook of workplace well-being* (pp. 1–44). Springer.

Kumar, V., & Modi, S. (2022). Leading in new VUCA environment: Role of positive leadership through spiritual and ethical values. In S. Dhiman & J.

Marques (Eds.), *Leadership after COVID-19*. Future of Business and Finance. Springer. https://doi.org/10.1007/978-3-030-84867-5_31

Long, S. D. (2008). *The perverse organization and its deadly sins*. Karnac Books.

Long, S. D. (2009). Greed. *Psychodynamic Practice, 15*(3), 245–259. https://doi.org/10.1080/14753630903024465

Martela, F., & Steger, M. F. (2016). The meaning of meaning in life: Coherence, purpose and significance as the three facets of meaning. *Journal of Positive Psychology, 11*(5), 531–545.

Mascaro, N., & Rosen, D. H. (2005). Existential meaning's role in the enhancement of hope and prevention of depressive symptoms. *Journal of Personality, 73*, 985–1014.

Maslow, A. H. (1943). A theory of human motivation. *Psychological Review, 50*(4), 370–396.

Maslow, A. H. (1970). *Motivation and personality* (2nd ed.). Harper & Row.

May, D., Gilson, R., & Harter, L. (2004). The psychological conditions of meaningfulness, safety and availability and the engagement of the human spirit at work. *Journal of Occupational and Organizational Psychology, 77*, 11–37.

Mitroff, I. I., & Denton, E. A. (1999). *A spiritual audit of corporate America*. Jossey-Bass.

Ricard, M. (2008). *Happiness: A guide to developing life's most important skill*. Atlantic Books Ltd. Little, Brown and Company.

Ricard, M. (2013). *Altruism: The power of compassion to change yourself and the world*. Atlantic Books.

Ricard, M. (2018). *Personal communication with author* (An Unpublished Source).

Robertson, A. F. (2001). *Greed: Gut feelings, growth, and history*. Polity Press.

Ryan, R. M., & Deci, E. L. (2001). On happiness and human potential: A review of research on hedonic and eudaimonic well-being. *Annual Review of Psychology, 52*, 141–166.

Ryff, C. D., & Singer, B. (2003). Flourishing under fire: Resilience as a prototype of challenged thriving. In C. L. M. Keyes & J. Haidt (Eds.), *Flourishing: Positive psychology and life well lived*. Washington: American Psychological Association.

Sen, S. (2014). *Personal communication with author* (An Unpublished Source).

Sreedharan, E. (2017). In R. B. Aklekar, *India's railway man—A biography of E. Sreedharan*. Rupa.

Sreedharan, E. (2019). *Personal communication with author* (An Unpublished Source).

Steger, M. F., Frazier, P., Oishi, S., & Kaler, M. (2006). The meaning in life questionnaire: Assessing the presence of and search for meaning in life. *Journal of counseling psychology, 53*(1), 80.

Steger, M. F. (2012). Experiencing meaning in life: Optimal functioning at the nexus of well-being, psychopathology and spirituality. In P. T. P. Wong (Ed.), *The human quest for meaning* (2nd ed., pp. 165–184). Routledge.

Steger, M. F., Kashdan, T. B., Sullivan, B. A., & Lorentz, D. (2008). Understanding the search for meaning in life: Personality, cognitive style, and the dynamic between seeking and experiencing meaning. *Journal of Personality, 76*(2), 199–228.

Steger, M. F., Dik, B. J., & Duffy, R. D. (2012). Measuring meaningful work: The work and meaning inventory (WAMI). *Journal of career Assessment, 20*(3), 322–337.

Swami Parmarthananda. (2003). *Lectures on The Bhagavad Gita* (Vol. I). The Samskrita Academy.

Swami Parmarthananda. (2014). *Personal communication with author* (An Unpublished Source).

Ward, S. J., & King, L. A. (2017). Work and good life: How work contributes to meaning in life. *Research in Organizational Behavior, 37*, 59–82.

Yadav, S. (2019). *Personal communication with author* (An Unpublished Source).

CHAPTER 5

The Reference to Contemplative Indian Traditional Wisdom of Flourishing and Fulfillment Regarding the Organizational Workplace

Nidhi Kaushal

Abstract The segment of the organization's behavior has an immense and valuable role in the context of flourishment and well-being, which determines the responsibility of the leader to tend to the effective participation of its workers and their ability to sustain organizational changes. The worthy considerable traditional wisdom contained in Indian folklore has always been full of its teachings, policies, and morals, which reflects its implication in the field of organizational development through the perspective of psychological wellness and prosperity. It has a zenith elegance of personality enrichment through the aspect of values and humanity and is helpful in equipping the organizational people with the qualities of self-leadership through self-transformation, perspective shifts, a new visionary approach, group morale, and the skill of managing the

N. Kaushal (✉)
Indian Institute of Technology Roorkee, Roorkee, India

77

change. This chapter highlights the significance of ethical as well as contemplative wisdom and its efficacy and cogency in identifying the strategies and measures for the leaders in the modern organizational system.

Keywords Employee engagement · Flourishment · Group morale · Happiness · Self-leadership · Vision · Mindful management · Perspective shifts

INTRODUCTION

Scholars have significantly affirmed that many unique creations of literary works have been found in Indian traditions, systems, and local histories, which are available as a unique contribution of literature in the form of complete books or treatises, and are valuable in gaining insight and wisdom required for the transformation in life. Wisdom is reading the patterns of life with discernment and applying insight with integrity and care (Strom, 2013). Indian social milieu is very culture-oriented and complex (Balasubramanian, 2007), and ancient wisdom is the knowledge and insight derived from ancient texts (Low, 2014), while collective wisdom refers to knowledge and the insight gained from group and community interaction (Briskin & Erickson, 2009). Leadership has been conceived as the focus of certain group practices, like compliance, authority, behavior, coercion, synergy, and interaction (Bass, 2007), and the wisdom of leadership has an extensive scope because it is beyond the individualistic or materialistic outlook that exerted positive effects on all areas of the organization (Yang, 2011).

Wisdom deliberately encompasses the aspect of happiness, which propounds the insights on achieving well-being morally and altruistically (Gotise & Upadhyay, 2018). It makes people aware of their ability to deal with problems and solve them and engages them consciously to think and act afresh (Subramoney, 2020). The field of well-being and happiness discloses the secrets of psychological wealth because happiness is a part of well-being and underlines cultural and cognitive elements of people (Tandon, 2016). Values have implications for the fulfillment of work or life achievements, which determines the well-being of a person and makes his life worthful (Tiberius, 2018). The driving forces of strong aspirations stimulate the abilities within the individual, and this talent growth leads to perfection. Fulfillment connects the work to a sense of meaning and purpose and shows the leader's committed engagement and responsiveness, and he has the potential to fulfill the interests of the workers through self-realization and moral goodness and conducting the work with dignity (Gewirth, 2009).

Change emerges when power transforms from one coalition to another, and a new combination of ideologies and values gains ascendancy (Smith & Graetz, 2011) because employees, the projects team, and executives have different priorities, knowledge, and motivation, and the change brings all these set of terms together in a potentially volatile mix (Hiatt & Creasey, 2003). A leader who has the strength to influence and change people's psychology has different goals and priorities, and his performance is scrutinized by compatible measures and recognized with rewards (Cohen & Bradford, 2011). Vision plays a key role in providing useful change by helping to direct, align, and inspire the actions of group members (Kotter, 2012), and it helps to synthesize, vocalize, and translate their aspirations as well (Fairholm, 2000). Every individual has a passion, and the vision is the application of that passion (Balasubramanian, 2007), and a leader's self-confidence determines his ability to succeed in diverse fields of work (Cohen, 2009). The art of leadership involves visualizing the future and aligning and inspiring people with that vision (Kotter, 2012). It has been perceived as a requirement to focus on creating and sustaining the vision, catalyzing alignment, and encouraging learning, exploration, and creativity (Adams, 2005).

Work fulfillment is usually satisfactory and involves the development of aptitude and basic tendencies. (Feinberg, 2020), and it includes meaningful and purpose-driven work as well as meeting the challenges and growth perspective. Work fulfillment, satisfaction, and the doer's flourishing, upliftment, and well-being are interrelated aspects that embellish the dignity and prosperity of the workplace. A person develops through his satisfaction in his work and certainly considers it important regarding his wellness and also further leads to better performance and expected benefits. Every individual has the potential to create more happiness than the condition of suffering by improving mindsets, viewpoints, and reactions to every action. Making the state of one's mind ideal for every situation is essential in achieving happiness and includes winning the struggle over fear and misery and developing an inner support system. This chapter has been described in five parts which idealize the scenario of contemplative traditional wisdom-based policies of the leader, such as (1) The Significance of Wisdom in the Concept of Perspective Shifts; (2) Inference of Visionary Approach of the Leader for Employee Engagement and Self-Transformation; (3) Wisdom as a Prerequisite Virtue of the Leader to Develop Group Morale for Well-Being; (4) Sustaining Change and Development in the Organization by Mindful Management; (5) The Strategy of Self-Leadership for Empowerment and Workplace Flourishment.

LITERATURE

Happiness is the state of mind that we have the power to control and that control lies with our thinking (Bristol & Horowitz, 2018). The field of sporting activities has included several metaphors for examining patterns of winning and losing and seeing the elements of exceptional leadership and teamwork (Kanter, 2008). There are two sides to every business, the human and the material, and the best achievement is possible only when both are interwoven into one harmonious whole (Muller, 2000). Under good leadership, even a venture with many shortcomings can succeed (Srinivasan, 2006). Leadership is something you either have or don't have the effort to use experience for development (Mccall, 2010). Sophisticated psychology locates psychological characteristics within people and people within their settings broadly construed (Peterson & Seligman, 2004). Trust and goodwill have flourished only at that organization or place, where fair structures are available to protect rights and foster responsibilities (Hromek & Walsh, 2011).

The cognitive conflict has the potential for constructive change (DiPaola, 2003), and this change has been used positively to improve the environment for leadership (Briggs, 2003). The literature on management has always recognized the leader's role, particularly related to motivation (Mintzberg, 1989). Leaders create corporate spirit, a spiritual force that honors high performance, compassion, empathy for others, and individual corporation (Fairholm, 2000). They need to make sense of experience for themselves and others (Luthans, 2010). Reflective leadership has considered being transformative as long as it builds success in other people by reducing barriers while implementing leadership behavior for change (Gökar & Bozkus, 2017). Committed, responsible, and inspiring leaders have created a culture of care, which leads to the qualitative service of the organization (Cockerell, 2010). A change in the socio-economic setup invariably brings a change in the cultural fabric (Sen, 2004). Building enterprises capable of continually adapting to changing realities clearly demands new ways of thinking and operating (Senge, 2010). Reinforcement is only possible when every transformation has been effectively implemented in the organization (Hiatt, 2006). Genuine care for organizational goals proves the credibility and integrity of the employees (Cohen & Bradford, 2011). The ultimate responsibility of leaders is to ensure that the organization has the ability to remain functional in fast-changing circumstances (Holbeche, 2010).

Change leadership engages in strategic and tactical planning to make the most of the moment to strengthen team members (Wallin, 2010). Mentoring or instructing is a process of engagement, and learning is its fundamental purpose (Marquardt & Loan, 2006). Organizational development has emerged from applied social psychology and education and learning for a grown person in the early 1960s as a process for helping organizations solve problems and more fully realize their potential (Adams, 2005). The real strength of any organization is not derived from a monolithic, dictatorial system of management but from the management of a multiplicity of perspectives that are useful and valuable (Axelrod, 2008). Leadership is a universal phenomenon in individuals (Bass, 2007), and institutionalizing a leadership-centered culture is the ultimate act of leadership (Kotter, 2007). A leader should be open to learning from people's insight and efforts at every level (Stephan & Pace, 2002). The hero innovator (leader) is the naturally gifted individual (or organization) who brings about innovation through talent, grit, determination, and single-minded devotion to the goal (Denning et al., 2010).

Stories help to make sense of past events and perspective the future, where storytelling is an ancient and classical way of imparting the wisdom of the culture (Sole & Wilson, 2002). They are influential and productive in extending the business by developing and initiating an effective marketing strategy from their insight. Likewise, Myths give meaning to a complex system and transmit a sense of cultural values to guide people's behavior. Leaders should take advantage of resourceful mutual benefit partnering and create opportunities to thrive in a world of shape-shifting organizations, which provide flexible ways of developing business and social value (Johansen, 1992). Those with high strategic power can make better decisions and reduce disruptions through harmonizing and synergizing team members' strengths (Rath & Conchie, 2009).

Leaders in transformational leadership experience prevalent conflict while carrying out their responsibilities and caregiving obligations in the organizations (Markham, 1999). Great leaders have observed that staying focused is the key to the success of managerial disciplines and improving creativity (Eich, 2008). They instill grit in followers for their goal of performance enhancement and the good of humanity they endeavor (Sutton, 2010). Charismatic leaders lead with a vision that arises from appropriate analysis because they are sincere, emphatic, and credible and sacrifice their self-interest (House et al., 2013). Inclusive leaders consciously take calculated risks through their susceptibility and authenticity and archetype the behavior of followers (Brown, 2019).

Self-fulfillment is experienced with the nature of interaction with personal and inner identity because thoughts reflect pure consciousness to experience itself, and awareness leads to mental well-being (Sirshree, 2018). Well-being and happiness show the ethical nature of the person and lead to his value fulfillment through achieving goals (Tiberius, 2018). One should make alignment with his values to make them effectively applicable in the social environment to live with responsibility because optimism influences holistic well-being (Subramoney, 2020). Morale is the group spirit to get success where participants work better to contribute significantly toward the organizational mission (Bowles & Cooper, 2009). In an organizational environment, members feel an emotional connection with the group due to high morale and satisfaction factors (Mehrotra, 2005). Group morale also depends upon the leadership style in which the democratic leader has more morale in respect of the authoritarian style, and time perspective has also played a vital role in it, in which past events, future planning, and a feeling of security in the present comes (Suleman, 2008).

The Significance of Wisdom in the Concept of Perspective Shifts

Wisdom implies the ability of humans to make wise judgments and be sensible about their prospective outcomes (Briskin & Erickson, 2009), and in terms of good leadership, leadership designed to build enduring organizations and worthwhile enterprises requires rules, policies, and laws that connect with reality in genuinely productive and ethical ways, that guide and make possible actions and behavior likely to contribute to the prosperity of the common endeavor (Axelrod, 2008). Practical wisdom is an essential foundation of leadership in organizational functioning

(Krahnke et al., 2014), because the function of leadership is to produce change, and setting the direction of that change is fundamental to leadership (Kotter, 2007), and the experiential knowledge contained in practical wisdom enables people to make ethical judgments (Nonaka & Takeuchi, 2011). Good contextual intelligence broadens the bandwidth of leaders to develop and adapt strategies for different situations (Nye, 2008) because wisdom defines progress as a state of proficiency without experience and insight, which comes from the essence of a person (Stebbins, 2015).

A wise leader makes judgments and takes actions amid the constant flux of work, constantly creates opportunities for employees to mutual learning, coordinates and spurs them to act, synthesizes everyone's knowledge, and strives to understand all the contradictions in human nature like good or bad, civility, optimism, diligence, negligence, etc. (Nonaka & Takeuchi, 2011). Value is a worthy concept (Kanzunnudin et al., 2018), and a leader must have genuine character, godly courage, and a compassionate spirit (Ekeke, 2007). True Leaders are always consistent and uniform in their words and deeds and exhibit morality (Gardner, 2013). They fulfill human resources' conventional responsibilities ethically to advance their organization's fortune (Holbeche, 2010). With the spirit of truth-telling, they provide an insular view of reality and make decision-making a collaborative process (Markham, 1999).

The concept of perspective shifts has a significant role in the attitudinal transformation of employees because the particularity of attitudes acts as the resistance of making any amendments for a brighter future. The change process has involved emotional content because nobody likes to surrender the comfort associated with the status quo or what they value (Issah, 2018), and making an advancement or shift from this kind of engagement represents leadership with emotional intelligence. Organizational change activities have examined the complexities of the systematic framework, which assert that transformation is the result of several interconnected causes and effects of an analytical framework (Amagoh, 2008), and through which a leader recognizes the possibilities of enhancing the performance and capabilities of his group members. The explicit nature of the person enables him to achieve the target enthusiastically (Evans, 2013), and experience the merits of that change in life (Sablonnière et al., 2013). Changes in the value happen due to the functioning of certain short-term and long-term forces of the external and internal environment of the organization (Abramson & Inglehart, 2009).

Leadership has analyzed as the personal style or demeanor of a nominal head and specifies the influence and power of the leader (Vecchio, 2007), and a liberal attitude toward its group members creates goodwill and support for the leader, which is beneficial in organizational growth (Srinivasan, 2006), and a leadership team aims to form a purposeful community for the sake of others (Heuser & Shawchuck, 2010). Literary scholars have observed, analyzed, and acknowledged "the concept of change" through folktales and highlighted their psychological impressions on the mindfulness of people through listening or reading the tales. The application of insightful leadership is the most prominent requirement of the present time, and the process of change, its outcome, and its impact have been identified through leadership-based literary compositions. Therefore, a folktale regarding the awareness and wisdom of a thoughtful leader is given here.

The king of Vijayanagara (a city in South India) was a prosperous and kind person. Once, he thought of distributing gold coins and gems, without any context, among the people. He wanted to show his lavish lifestyle and wealth esteem. He asked Tenali Rama (the minister in his court) to accompany him during this occasion and look after the expensive jewels. Eventually, on the way during the journey, the bag full of gems exploded, and they started falling. But the minister, despite being a wise man, did not complain to the king because he was only asked to "notice" and not to "tell."

After going some distance, the king saw a pond, stopped to bathe in it, and started chanting Hare Rama. In his native language Kannada, the word "Hare" was meant to be to tear, and "Rama" was the name of the minister, so, by listening to his order, he tore off all the king's clothes. On being asked, he replied that he was following his orders as he did while gems were falling. Incidentally, his activity awakened him, and he realized that he was wasting his wealth in an impractical way and without any motive. He felt regretful for what he did and again praised his minister for his observation and awareness. In this way, the minister acted as a true leader, performed his assignment candidly, and established his identity as a wise leader (Board, 2013).

Leadership wisdom has based on integrity, which includes powerful core principles for goal-achievement, and is influential in identifying the attributes of developing the character required for sustaining the leadership tactics. In this saying, the wise minister not only used his wisdom to put a stop to vain-full expenses incurred by the king but also gave the lesson of prudence, coherence, and wealth management by changing his perspective toward abundance. This story is useful for a leader to understand the principle of perspective shift. A person is identified as a leader by the group when he believes to be trustworthy and significantly fulfills his responsibilities in changing the present circumstances and sustaining the positive development at the organizational, societal, or national level. He should be aware and loyal to perform his given commitments sincerely but also know the rational use of organizational resources, which is his utmost duty to control and check on venture-related activities. The perspective shift signifies unidentified opportunities and enhances the competence and confidence level of the people through transparent and accurate means.

Motivation and cognition are the conceptual constructs for the change, and his social psychological perspective reflects the cognitive behavior of the leader for that development (Sinatra & Dole, 1998), which sees the change as the main aspiration of the leader from a psychological perspective (Train et al., 2007). Characteristics of social exchange have a significant impact on the appraisal of organizational change (Michel & Gonzalez-Morales, 2013), which helps to set the procedure for further prospective advancements in the organization. Perspective change involves a process that renders the ambivalence of different perspectives (Brockmole & Wang, 2002), which acts as a foundation to change events or personalities at a fundamental level. Perceptions of the people include the influence of their faith-based beliefs and traditional practices (Miller-Perrin & Mancuso, 2014), and shifts in their attitudes provide a wider scope of the phenomenon to them.

Changes in perception through proper brainstorming and analysis of situations modify one's thinking and enhance knowledge paving the way for new opportunities. Through perspective shifts, even a very difficult problem gets solved smoothly, and this mechanism works efficiently for implementing the measures or strategy of well-being and flourishment in the organization or workplace. A true leader always wants the suitableness and wellness of his organization and its workers, by all means, so he conducts the organization's work through proper coordination and empowers them skilfully through his wisdom and vision. Thus, the approach to shift in perspective with the wisdom of development or improvement in the circumstances can serve as a notable aspect in the motive of workplace well-being.

Inference of Visionary Approach of the Leader for Employee Engagement and Self-Transformation

The quality of a strong vision implies an accurate assessment of the present activities and their future related prospects, which reflects an excellent attribute of a wise leader. It also introduces his mental strength and the effect of positive psychology. Leadership for change demands inspiration (Heifetz et al., 2009) and achieving the highest aspirations with a visionary approach (Luthans, 2010), including perspective shifts and innovative ideas (Patterson, 2017). The leader at work is a fighter who wants to be a warrior (Chatterjee, 2012). He challenges his followers to excellence, helps to increase their talents for the sake of both the team and the individual, relates to organizational goals, and acts as a mood setter as well as a task giver (Fairholm, 2000). The galvanizing process of development is synchronized by leadership, as social and political, which prepares the leader to accept the challenge of change (Sen, 2004). Powerful leadership has based on the philosophy of the nobleness of the human spirit and soul, which has the potential to change people with persistence (Stephan & Pace, 2002). Indigenous wisdom is an attitude, belief (ideology), the time-tested ability of values, traditions, norms, and ethics (Kanzunnudin et al., 2018). Strong leadership requires wisdom that has been enacted at the moment of the time (Smythe & Norton, 2011), so it is an act that is consciously tried (Balasubramanian, 2007).

The purpose of life develops during people's existence in the world, which has been discovered and rediscovered and becomes a sense of joy (Leider, 2008). The principles of psychology have a major contribution to recognizing the potential of change in leadership (Hiatt & Creasey, 2003). A leader's ability to deal with complexity and differences requires a novel or developed leadership behavior, which includes an unbounded vision and skills to function efficiently (Gundling, 2011). Anderson and Anderson (2002) define that if the required behavior and style change are significantly employed, then people's mindsets have also changed effectively. Building positive relations is the key to effective leadership (DiPaola, 2003). The approach to change is efficacious in humanity, building knowledge, skills, and motivation, and establishing and maintaining positive relationships (Hromek & Walsh, 2011).

Stories are literary creations filled with human qualities and include the power of understanding the human personality, implementing morality, solving issues, and maintaining the belief system of local cultural traditions. A thoughtful leader's truth, honesty, self-confidence, wisdom, positive psychology, and cultural ideology have certainly been helpful in making noteworthy changes in the organization because he is significantly determined and strengthens and executes his goals through these virtues, along with reinforcement. A folktale describing the positive psychological perspective and visionary strength of a change-bound leader has given here:

Matadin was an Indian farmer who had five sons, but these five boys used to fight with each other. Even on small matters, they used to quarrel and scrimmage. He was very concerned with the fight of his boys, so he called them one day with the idea of convincing them, and for that, he had already made a small bundle of five thin and dry twigs. He asked his sons to break the bundle of these twigs and win the prize. But all five boys started quarreling to break the bundle first to win the prize.

Then the farmer told them to let the younger brother break it. He lifted the bundle and tried to exert a lot of pressure on it, but he did not succeed and gave it to his elder brother. He too pressed it very hard but could not break. In this way, all the boys took the bundle and tried hard, but nobody got succeeded. At that moment, the farmer opened the bundle and gave each twig to all the boys, and this time everyone broke the twigs very quickly. Then he explained that as long as these branches were together, no one could break them, but when they split apart, they get broken easily.

Similarly, if they keep fighting with each other, others will be teased and suppress them. But, if they live together, then no one will dare to enmity with them. On the same day, the Matadin boys gave up fighting and started living together cordially (Poddhar, 1950).

In this way, the farmer changed the mindset of his sons through his power of positive psychology and practical wisdom and taught them a lesson of unity. This folktale reveals the importance of positive psychology in transformative affairs, and it is very important to have solidarity and coherence among people of the group or in the organization. Cooperation and benevolence are very important traits required for a valued transformation that also strengthen the leader's character and vision. The leadership profile includes his competent characteristic, and he should have established a correlation between the practices and procedures at the workplace for securing the tact of fruitful development in the organization. He should motivate his employees with the development of positivism, for organizational welfare, by the practice of his change-leadership strategy.

Likewise, a strong vision is the reflection of future planning that makes the leader mentally strong and conscious to face challenges and difficulties and defines its prospects. It represents the futuristic favorable state of an organization, which gets communicated through the corresponding organizational vision statement, which acts as a critical factor in prospective success (Jantz, 2017). Visionary leaders maintain organizational effectiveness with their efficient leadership skills (Taylor et al., 2014), by significantly affecting the organizational behavior of employees. They influence followers to experience a shared sense of the organization's ultimate goal with the approach of rhetoric, shared cognition, visions, and values, thereby boosting coordination and performance (Carton, 2014). Transformation-oriented visionary leadership has the utmost significance to awake and drive the inner strength of employees to invigorate and inspire their potential rendering into actions, and to make required transformations for business survival and growth in today's turbulent environment (Dwivedi, 2006). Therefore, developing the capability of visionary strength through experience and analysis is very necessary for a leader in employee engagement, which is also beneficial to improve the present conditions to make futuristic strategies of benefit.

The initiative to change oneself, whether it is psychological, personal, internal, or external, leads to making a transformation in others as well. The aspects of well-being include the fulfillment of work and flourishment and are coordinated by the approaches of the leader, and he implements every possible tactic to sustain it in the organization, whether to make a transformation at his personal or emotional level. Because as he performs, everyone approves of him, and in this process, he often has to be taken challenging and exceptional decisions for the good of all, which in the long run provide direction, speed, and growth to everyone.

Wisdom as a Prerequisite Virtue of the Leader to Develop Group Morale for Well-Being

Wisdom includes acumen and deliberately grouping with wise people, which makes leaders learners of practical experience (Bandelli, 2021). The path of observing the truth unfolds the complex conditions because it sets the state of an organization on new paradigms founded on constant transformations and beyond any condition of equilibrium, overbalance, or even unbalance (Markham, 1999). The development of quintessential culture in a group requires openness and trust from leaders in their leadership (Schein & Schein, 2018) because trust has been verified and applied by human races when a task, activity, or relationship comes to an end (Eich, 2008). The character gets enriched over the understanding of ethics, while wisdom evokes guiding principles for life's purposes (Beebe, 2011).

Wisdom is knowledge of what is true or right, coupled with good judgment (Ekeke, 2007), and ancient wisdom supplies the values for strengthening leadership (Low, 2014). The process of developing it requires us to integrate the heart into our experience (Stebbins, 2015). The development of Judgmental ability has been attained by individuals through expertise in liberal arts, such as philosophy, history, and literature (Nonaka & Takeuchi, 2011). Kindness is a value in leadership that enables a leader to execute with the power of his virtues for the personal or organizational benefits and their significance of national or global value (Haskins & Thomas, 2018), while humanity offers the perspective of developing shared concepts of civilizations based on human global governance (Gill, 2011). Prosperity includes the strength of hopes and aspirations that courageously displays leadership and is nurtured through the leader's relentless will (Ziegler, 2010). Human beings have learned to cooperate because connectedness shows a positive tie between the individual and the social entity of belongingness (Dragolov et al., 2016).

Leadership is a collective and sensible endeavor that implies varied learning modes to idealize complex concepts, like the Indian spiritual leaders have commended and included the cultural and traditional approach of *Satsanga* in their leadership learning, which emphasizes creating harmony and respect for humanity (Starkey & Hall, 2012). Learning is a development of valuable affinity, which stimulates the person or group toward more awareness, mindfulness, and decision power, while experiential learning means gaining knowledge through action where discussions have turned experiences into wisdom (Riddle et al., 2015). Wise Leaders often interconnect with beliefs of various cultures, and their folklore provides a mechanism to learn the perspective of group strategy and its management through a narrative approach, and the development through learning implicates the interaction of abilities and relationships of members and organizational systems and reciprocation over each other.

A group is defined as an assemblage of people who share the feeling of being together in which the leader and the group act as a social unit (Mehrotra, 2005). Trust and confidence are essential factors of group morale, which underlines attitude and a sense of purpose, including proper internal communication to develop good team spirit (Adair, 2010). Organizational-related significant information instead of irrelevant stuff has a positive effect on the group morale, which enhances the zeal and zest of the members to pursue their tasks (Klein, 2013). Morale is the feeling of overcoming any obstacle with the aim of goodness which retains the perspective of well-being (Ambler & Burnett, 1966). It is the state of mind and action. High morale indicates discipline, obedience, unity, and less disappointment to maintain a level of enthusiasm in the behavior of group members (Sharma & Sharma, 2004). It develops a sense of psychological well-being among them, which enhances their skills in Management (Bowles & Cooper, 2009).

Group morale reflects the sense of happiness and bliss of its members. Positive factors play a significant role in its context, where positive goals are essential for the good morale of the employees because a clear and definite goal creates solidity in the group. There is a mutual relationship between aspiration level and achievement level in determining group morale, and for its higher level, the members must realize that they are moving toward achieving their goals and this group is successful in fulfilling their auxiliary needs. Equality of sacrifice and gain within-group affect group morale where the feeling of solidarity and identification is an emotional factor that makes the morale high or low. The involvement or participation in group activity enhances the identification of group people, which raises their morale, and being embodied in group action reduces mental conflict because of more introspection or identification (Suleman, 2008).

Folklore has resonant and powerful features (Heifetz et al., 2009), and it is a dynamic component of culture with the capacity to adapt to situations of social and cultural changes (Sen, 2004). This form of creative literature has contributed to ethnic consciousness through which an indigenous group identified itself regarding others (Jayaraj, 2004), and from this, a tale has been identified to explore the significance of group morale toward the flourishment of the organization and fulfillment of its members.

One time in an Indian farmer's field, some of his laborers used to do his work of cultivation and plantation. One day that group was doing the work of weeding and hoeing, and after working for an hour, all the members would sit for a while, relax, talk, and start working again. In the meantime, their master (the farmer) used to work with his trowel and other types of equipment. When they saw him working, then they also joined him, and it became their routine practice in the fields. When it was noon time, he went to the laborers and said to stop work, eat food, and take some rest. They, too, would soon come back and stick to their work.

After some time, seeing his farm work doubled, his neighbor asked him why his field had more growth though he provided breaks to the workers and did not scold them, while he used to chase his laborers for every small task. He said that he gives priority to more affection and sympathy than strictness in the policy of taking work from others, and that's why they performed with full dedication, and therefore fieldwork is done better and in abundance. He is always sincerely concerned for the well-being and fulfillment of his workers by keeping their group morale at a high level and encouraging them toward happiness, which makes prosperity remain in his workplace, and he gets the expected benefits (Khemka & Lakkad, 2020).

This tale meaningfully indicates the implication of group morale in workplace well-being and flourishment. A member's morale not only enhances his efficiency but also directly positively affects the group and organizational work, respectively. It is the responsibility of the leader that he should take care of the psychological well-being and happiness of all people for organizational flourishing and productivity. His inherent wisdom enables him to regulate the activities all around and employ the potential of his members in an accurate way. So, developing and maintaining group morale is a must by the leader for influential organizational functioning, which represents the harmony and cooperative spirit enduring in the members toward achieving a common goal through collective working.

Sustaining Change and Development in the Organization by Mindful Management

Management practices are always context-bound (Martin, 2006), and good management is the rule of the rational mind, which unites individuals in effective cooperation (Robertson, 2000). An entrepreneur's role has described the manager as the voluntary initiator of change

(Mintzberg, 1989), so as a change manager, he focuses on the objectives as a way of facilitating interpersonal alignment between participants in the organization (Pollack & Algeo, 2015). Likewise, a leader is a goal-driven person who mobilizes and influences team members that willingly follow him (Barna, 1998). The secret to thriving organizational change involves his visionary outlook on employees' flourishment (Hiatt, 2006). The change leader must be a thoughtful and continuous reviewer and observer of the changes made and reflect as well as communicate about those transformations openly among the group (Wallin, 2010). Managing change is very important, and only leadership has the power to emphasize and stimulate employees' behavior significantly toward the organization's culture (Kotter, 2012).

An organization's culture has made up of its folklore, rituals, group norms, and protocols (Heifetz et al., 2009). Transformation or change is important for human consciousness and is also required at the organizational level and global level to live life more effectively (Adams, 2005). An enabling organizational structure encourages innovation, the expression of new ideas, and improvement in the group people (DiPaola, 2003), while the implementation of the change requires collective actions from the group people (Kotter, 2012) because organizational growth is associated with workers' development (Marquardt & Loan, 2006). Encouraging and empowering fellow workers for their contribution to the organizational work enhance their morale and productivity, which makes the transformation operational and functional (Stephan & Pace, 2002). A leadership style that is pace-setting and driving rather than devolved has been seen as promoting purposeful liaison between executives (Briggs, 2003).

People work harder when there is mutual trust, respect, concern for each other, and mutual integrity among the group members as human beings (Fairholm, 2000). Coordinating the efforts and gaining cooperation by the power of influence are significant aspects of contemporary work-life (Cohen & Bradford, 2011). Bronner (2009) finds that the technical way of thinking affects the conceptualization of tradition on the internet, while the folk internet is analytical in its structure rather than relational. A person is a product of his thoughts (Schwartz, 2014). He executes the task with significant visionary ideas, develops it with action, and makes progress because his subconscious mind always obeys a clear and ethically given order (Bristol & Horowitz, 2018). Communication comes in both words and deeds (Kotter, 2012), and folk narratives have integral power to communicate cultural integrity, forces, and standards, apparently for developing moral education among the local people (Blank, 2009). They are a powerful form of credible commutation that has captured employees' hearts and minds in an effective way. Living by inner truth means putting truth into practice (Fairholm, 2000), and the field of folklore has evolved as a discipline of literature to recognize the facts of enlightenment and is very effective in learning the process of social structures of traditional cultures (Sen, 2004). Cogliser (2003) finds that stories can foster imagination power among individuals and help them to develop their expressions of leadership.

The distinct feature of leadership includes the engagement of tasks with a liberal but rational attitude in a global-networking world, like the art of bringing the patches of fabric into an alliance to allow a big picture to emerge, which generates new meaning for the individuals (Einzig, 2017). Among the various forms of management studies, the field of change management has emerged as a source of learning the practices to manage people's resistance (Anderson & Anderson, 2010). The change is positive in many ways, but it also has a negative aspect because sometimes the changing environment and the outcome have not proved to be beneficial for everyone, and they are not accepted wholeheartedly, and this contradictory situation gives rise to conflict. Hiatt and Creasey (2003) observe that not managing the people side of change impacted the success of leaders and introduced risks into their ventures. Conflicts handled cooperatively and systematically during the change implementation process yield positive outcomes, develop insight, and strengthen the individuals emotionally, while competitively perpetuating the conflict results in wasting of energy (DiPaola, 2003).

A relevant instance of change and mindful management is presented here with respect to workplace well-being and fulfillment. During the freedom struggle in India, Mahatma Gandhi was a victim of the suppression of the British government of that time, and he had to stay in South Africa those days. The dictator general there repeatedly tried to break his confidence by sending him to jail, and at one time, he imprisoned him with a cobbler to humiliate him. But he knew the skill to make good use of the time and take advantage of the prevailing situation, so while in jail, he learned to make shoes from that prisoner. When he was released from prison, he presented a box to the dictator, which contained a pair of shoes for him. He felt amazed by his humility, despite his rude behavior toward him, and got overwhelmed by seeing his courtesy. He asked him why he did so. Then he said that everyone should have to make good use of adverse circumstances and implied his wisdom and skills because no human or work is small. Not only does the practice of mindful management of time or situation develops hidden aptitudes, but this factor also enriches the personality of the person and fulfills the component of well-being in the workplace (Khemka & Lakkad, 2020).

The aspects of change and development are enclosed with each other, which also indicates the way of management and control of the conditions in the organizational environment by the leader regarding the employees' flourishment. His mindfulness serves as the source of wisdom for synthesizing and analyzing events and providing efficacious outcomes, and this understanding enables him to employ fruitful strategical measures for significant organizational functioning. So, the insights from traditional wisdom, along with the life learning experiences of a leader, are valuable in the leadership pattern to sustain changes for the overall well-being.

The Strategy of Self-Leadership for Empowerment and Workplace Flourishment

Leadership is a cognitively socially constructed activity that includes the charisma and behavior of the followers for the positive effects of existing scripts and schemas (Shamir, 2006). The function of leadership can transform the organization into a learning institution by infusing the employees with moral values and a sense of meaningful purpose in working (Podolny et al., 2010). It is a multifaceted ethical relationship between people of the organization based on trust, obligation, and commitment, through which a leader imparts the moral significance of policies and actions to them (Ciulla, 2014). Its levels consist of the position, including foundation, consent about the mutual relationship of people, producing a harmonious environment, people empowerment, and pinnacle of legacy (Maxwell, 2011). The practice of leadership also observes the perspective of unsure matters and requires the quality of authenticity, which is an alignment between the beliefs, head, heart, and guts of the leader (Dotlich et al., 2009). It is not a function of position or status but rather an action. It is about affecting people in the way they are doing and believing (Black & Morrison, 2014). A leader dealing with diversity is more sensitive to differences and conflicts, so he should sustain an environment of transparency and authenticity for the followers to feel connected, unique, and rewarded, and not punished for slip-ups at the same time (Northouse, 2008).

Self-leadership engages team members through self-direction and motivation and is recognized as an antecedent of shared leadership, which reveals the team properties like team mindfulness, monitoring, reinforcement, reflexivity, and knowledge integration capability. It is associated with the dispersion of responsibility, group thinking, and social loafing in teams with low cognitive diversity. (Zhu et al., 2018). Leadership involves a way of life in-person that can be right or wrong depending on the responsive and proactive style of the leader (Banks et al., 2004), and its field is a theoretical and rigorous research exercise, while leadership itself is a process (Maxwell, 2011), and its value system consists of virtues, commandments of personal conduct, and morality (Ciulla, 2014). It uses persuasion and motivation processes to coordinate individuals collectively and enhances the conceptual skills of leaders to operate in the context of the organizational environment (Hunt & Fitzgerald, 2018). An effective leadership style transforms strategic thought into tactical plans (Ziegler, 2010). A high-performance expectation by the leader with his role modeling approach increases the collective efficacy of followers and stimulates them to make a full contribution to their organizational work (Cronin et al., 2015).

Folk tales are fiction with a dynamic spiritual account and have a significant place for learning about cultural inheritance (Huiyu, 2018), because they leave an indelible mark of morality on the mind, and develop a positive momentum in leadership. All morality-based compositions, whether they are poetry, articles, plays, or stories, reflect various human qualities like positive attitude, trust, patience, courage, truthfulness, honesty, etc. For example, the tales of *Panchatantra*, *Hitopadesha*, *Jātaka*, and other legends give a diverse introduction to the role of a leader in changing, encouraging, and sustaining human life. The composition of the story, which has based on the leadership theme, is helpful to individuals in gaining self-knowledge through the experiences of the leaders and also helpful in identifying the connections between the various connections of past and future practices. The morals of the folktales are like ethical statements that are helpful in the decision-making process for the leader. So a folktale from the ancient Indian treatise *Hitopadesha* describing the feature of self-leadership is given here:

Once, in a forest, a herd of elephants was suffering from thirst due to a lack of rain during the rainy season, and there was only water left for bathing small creatures. Then the lord of the herd went far away and found a pond full of clean water and showed the place to everyone. But small hares also lived on the banks of that pond, and every day the arrival of elephants crushed some of them.

But all the hares thought that if this herd of elephants kept on coming here every day and crushing them, it might be possible that their race would perish. Then an old hare among them consoled them and said that he would resolve this issue. He decided to mount the top of the hill to address the leader of the herd, and when that flock came to drink water, his chief asked him, who are you?

He replied that he is the messenger of the divine moon who speaks by his order that all the elephants have dispersed the hares (the guardians of the Moonlake), who have long been his proteges. After listening to him, the leader got horrified and accepted that it happened in ignorance and would not go there. The messenger said, if so, then pay homage to Lord Moon in the lake and please him, and then by taking him to the pond at night, the trembling image of the moon reflected in the water was shown, and he was bowed down. He apologized that he would not do so again, and with these words, he was sent away. In this way, if the rival is powerful or seems to be undefeated, then victory can be achieved by applying proper strategy with wisdom (Kale, 2015).

Sometimes, it becomes necessary for a leader to take the initiative in the given circumstances and act with his leadership potential rather than any directive organizational intake. In this tale, the hare not only saved the lives of other hares but also paved the way for their survival and well-being. He identified that their flourishment should be necessary for future growth and security and used his wisdom and vision to get rid of the elephants. In the challenging organizational environment, instead of losing hope, one must trust his belief system and identifies his leadership capabilities because then only the voice of the inner soul shows him the right direction.

Self-leadership includes conducting and managing without any other command, and this quality is found in optimistic people. In this approach, a person's inner soul motivates him, and he strives to help others through the perspective of selfless service. Such a person is often cheerful, contented, enthusiastic, and an influencer and acts as an inspiration to others. Purpose and passion operate together and constantly inspire exemplary leaders to make a significant difference in the present scenario apart from getting fame and fortune (Liu, 2010). Character establishes the conduct and fortune of the people, which is also prophetic in origin and determines prospective activities (Ciulla, 2014). A person's passion energizes and drives him toward his purpose and mission and gratifies his pleasures (Bandelli, 2021) because passion acts as fuel to energize an individual's direction and drives motivation, and is a key aspect of intuitive leadership (Porter-O'Grady & Malloch, 2009).

The visioning process is the process of moving from past events toward a new domain of the future, and its progression includes critical thinking, setting the target, following the right path, and sharing and celebrating success with the persons included (Bandelli, 2021). The leader has a primordial emotive function in a group that persuades everyone's emotions and maintains their even emotional state by avoiding over-enthusiasm and anxiety, which can affect their performance (Goleman et al., 2013). With his intelligence, creativity, knowledge, and expertise, he optimizes the synergy of people and flourishes their diversity to develop a socially harmonious work environment at a global level (Wibbeke, 2010). The encouraging manager should possess entrepreneurial characteristics and identify new opportunities, while the executing manager should be skilled in administrative competence and efficient use of resources (Piercy & Lane, 2009). Every employee has the potential to develop as a leader because leadership is demanded everywhere (Hays & Kim, 2012), so a leader can build organizational integrity with the collaboration of people with the same purpose, values, and ideals as one team (Harari, 2003). True leadership has prioritized the freedom to both "love and work" rather than any credential in life and makes the leader win because he prefers the common good over self-serving agendas (Eich, 2008).

Thus, the legacy of traditional wisdom in cultural practices and folklore of any region can serve as the means to explore and identify the relevant procedures for human flourishment and workplace well-being. India has rich ancient folk esteem as values and belief systems, stated in the form of treatises or tales and found to be fruitful with respect to the leadership and management policies in the modern organizational environment. A leader is always a lifelong learner who enriches his knowledge through experience and learning, and his members' happiness and satisfaction, and sustenance are vital to him, and the mechanism of gaining insights regarding organizational behavior from contemplative wisdom is persuasive and exemplary for him.

Conclusion

Happiness, fulfillment, and flourishment are consistent and serve as unified concepts in the organizational structure for the effective outcome of its procedures and practices. Despite various innovative trends and tactics, the inference of traditional wisdom is always universal and has been recognized through the study of related folklore or folktales. They have been found useful for analyzing and stating the phenomena of perspective shifts, self-transformation, employee engagement, group morale, and self-leadership in respect of categorizing and exploring the strategies and measures of workplace well-being. This chapter has an immense contribution toward specifying the importance of the wellness factor and its role in organizational functioning through examining the leader's policies based on wisdom in the context of employee flourishing. Mindful management is essential to sustain change and its enactment in the organization, along with the idealistic leadership of the leader. His accountability always counts and enriches his personality to retain the employees' optimism and responsiveness through appropriate and logical means.

Reference Questions

1. How can an effective change be brought in the working mechanism by unique intelligence and rational policies?
2. How the positive mindset and visionary leadership approach of a leader are effective in transforming behavior and enhancing the performance of workers?
3. Why is group morale necessary for constructive organizational operations and from the standpoint of employees' well-being?
4. How traditional wisdom and experience are helpful in managing and sustaining the change in the organization?
5. What is the inherent aspect of self-leadership, and how does this approach transforms an individual's personality as a leader?

Lessons

- The culmination of intelligence has a fundamental contribution to make the existing conditions conducive to the changing environment by the leader, which also has manifested as his efficacious aptitude.
- Learning from the folklore has demonstrated an effective criterion in changing the psychology of humans, and it presents a better human perspective based on prudence and benevolence.
- Morale is always necessary for pursuing any obligation, and in organizational tasks, group morale is the overall enthusiasm of every member, which has implications for work fulfillment.
- The skill of mindful management is necessary for the leader to imply the processes of wellness and flourishment regarding the utilization of every condition and available resource.
- Every person is a leader itself who exhibits leadership skills in the prevailing circumstances, so the concept of self-leadership has a crucial element of fulfilling accountability with the wisdom of a futuristic advantage.

References

Abramson, P. R., & Inglehart, R. F. (2009). *Value change in global perspective.* University of Michigan Press.

Adams, J. D. (2005). *Transforming work* (2nd ed.). Cosimo Inc.

Adair, J. (2010). *Effective motivation: How to get the best results from everyone.* Pan Macmillan.

Amagoh, F. (2008). Perspectives on organizational change: Systems and complexity theories. *The Innovation Journal: The Public Sector Innovation Journal, 13*(3), 1–14.

Ambler, R. K., & Burnett, E. R. (1966). *Morale level as a function of the subject's own definition of morale.* U.S. Naval Aerospace Medical Institute.

Anderson, D., & Anderson, L. A. (2002). *Beyond change management: Advanced strategies for today's transformational leaders.* John Wiley & Sons.

Anderson, D., & Anderson, L. A. (2010). *Beyond change management: How to achieve breakthrough results through conscious change leadership.* Wiley.

Axelrod, A. (2008). *Revolutionary management: John Adams on leadership.* Rowman & Littlefield.

Balasubramanian, S. (2007). *The art of business leadership: Indian experiences.* Sage.

Bandelli, A. C. (2021). *What every leader need: The ten universal and indisputable competencies of leadership effectiveness.* Covenant Books, Incorporated.

Banks, R. J., Ledbetter, B. M., & Pree, M. (2004). *Reviewing leadership (engaging culture): A Christian evaluation of current approaches.* Baker Publishing Group.

Barna, G. (1998). Nothing is more important than leadership. In G. Barna (Ed.), *Leaders on leadership: Wisdom, advice and encouragement on the art of leading god's people* (pp. 17–30). Gospel Light Publications.

Bass, B. M. (2007). Concepts of leadership. In R. P. Vecchio (Ed.), *Leadership: Understanding the dynamics of power and influence in organizations* (2nd ed., pp. 3–22). University of Notre Dame Press.

Beebe, G. D. (2011). *The shaping of an effective leader: Eight formative principles of leadership.* InterVarsity Press.

Black, J. S., & Morrison, A. J. (2014). *The global leadership challenge.* Routledge.

Blank, T. J. (2009). Introduction. Toward a conceptual framework for the study of folklore and the internet. In T. J. Blank (Ed.), *Folklore and the internet: Vernacular expression in a digital world* (pp. 1–20). University Press of Colorado.

Board, M. E. P. (2013). *151 stories of Tenali Raman.* Manoj Publications.

Bowles, D., & Cooper, C. (2009). *Employee morale: Driving performance in challenging times.* Palgrave Macmillan.

Briggs, A. R. J. (2003). Facilitating the role of middle managers in further education. In L. Kydd, L. Anderson, & W. Newton (Eds.), *Leading people and teams in education* (pp. 199–214). Sage.

Briskin, A., & Erickson, S. (2009). *The power of collective wisdom: And the trap of collective folly.* Berrett-Koehler Publishers.

Bristol, C. M., & Horowitz, M. (2018). *The magic of believing (condensed classics): The immortal program to unlocking the success-power of your mind.* Gildan Media LLC aka G&D Media.

Brockmole, J. R., & Wang, R. F. (2002). Changing perspective within and across environments. *Cognition, 87,* 59–67. https://doi.org/10.1016/S0010-0277(02)00231-7

Bronner, S. J. (2009). Digitising and virtualising folklore. In T. J. Blank (Ed.), *Folklore and the internet: Vernacular expression in a digital world* (pp. 21–66). University Press of Colorado.

Brown, J. (2019). *How to be an inclusive leader.* Berrett-Koehler Publishers.

Carton, A. M. (2014). A (blurry) vision of the future: How leader rhetoric about ultimate goals influences performance. *Academy of Management Journal, 57*(6), 1544–1570. https://doi.org/10.5465/amj.2012.0101

Chatterjee, D. (2012). *Timeless leadership: 18 leadership sutras from the Bhagavad Gita*. Wiley.

Ciulla, J. B. (2014). Leadership ethics: Expending the territory. In J. B. Ciulla (Ed.), *Ethics, the heart of leadership* (3rd ed., pp. 3–31). ABC-CLIO.

Cockerell, L. (2010). *Creating magic: 10 common sense leadership strategies from a life at Disney*. Random House.

Cohen, A. R., & Bradford, D. L. (2011). *Influence without authority*. Wiley.

Cohen, W. A. (2009). *Drucker on leadership: New lessons from the father of modern management*. Wiley.

Cogliser, C. C. (2003). "Teacher tell me a story": Using fiction in the leadership classroom. In R. Pillai & S. Stites-Doe (Eds.), *Teaching leadership: Innovative approaches for the 21st century* (pp. 31–56). IAP.

Cronin, L. D., Arthur, C. A., Hardy, J. T., & Callow, N. (2015). Transformational leadership and task cohesion in sport: The mediating role of inside sacrifice. *Journal of Sport and Exercise Psychology, 37*, 23–36.

Denning, P. J., Dunham, R., & Brown, J. S. (2010). *The innovator's way: Essential practices for successful innovation*. MIT Press.

DiPaola, M. F. (2003). Conflict and change: Daily challenges for school leaders. In N. Bennett, M. Crawford, & M. Cartwright (Eds.), *Effective educational leadership* (pp. 143–158). Sage.

Dotlich, D. L., Cairo, P. C., & Rhinesmith, S. H. (2009). *Leading in times of crisis: Navigating through complexity, diversity and uncertainty to save your business*. Wiley.

Dragolov, G., Ignácz, Z. S., Lorenz, J., Delhey, J., Boehnke, K., & Unzicker, K. (2016). *Social cohesion in the Western world: What holds societies together: Insights from the social cohesion radar*. Springer.

Dwivedi, R. (2006). Visionary leadership: A survey of literature and case study of Dr A.P.J. Abdul Kalam at DRDL. *Vision: The Journal of Business Perspective, 10*(3), 11–21. https://doi.org/10.1177/097226290601000302

Eich, D. P. (2008). *The F word: Good words for great leaders*. iUniverse.

Einzig, H. (2017). *The future of coaching: Vision, leadership and responsibility in a transforming world*. Routledge.

Ekeke, C. K. (2007). *Leadership wisdom*. Xulon Press.

Evans, I. M. (2013). *How and why people change foundations of psychological therapy*. Oxford University Press.

Fairholm, G. W. (2000). *Capturing the heart of leadership: Spirituality and community in the new American workplace*. Greenwood Publishing Group.

Feinberg, J. (2020). *Freedom and fulfillment: Philosophical essays*. Princeton University Press.

Gardner, W. L. (2013). Authentic leadership. In E. H. Kessler (Ed.), *Encyclopaedia of management theory* (pp. 53–56). Sage.

Gewirth, A. (2009). *Self-fulfillment*. Princeton University Press.

Gill, S. (2011). Introduction: Global crisis and the crisis of global leadership. In S. Gill (Ed.), *Global crises and the crisis of global leadership* (pp. 1–20). Cambridge University Press.

Gökar, S. D., & Bozkus, K. (2017). Reflective leadership: Learning to manage and lead human organizations. In A. Alvinius (Ed.), *Contemporary leadership challenges* (pp. 27–46). BoD—Books on Demand.

Goleman, D., Boyatzis, R. E., & McKee, A. (2013). *Primal leadership: Unleashing the power of emotional intelligence.* Harvard Business Review Press.

Gotise, P., & Upadhyay, B. K. (2018). Happiness from ancient Indian perspective: Hitopadeśa. *Journal of Happiness Studies, 19*, 863–879. https://doi.org/10.1007/S10902-017-9853-2

Gundling, E. (2011). *What is global leadership? 10 key behaviors that define great global leaders.* Nicholas Brealey Publishing.

Harari, O. (2003). *The leadership secrets of Colin Powell.* McGraw-Hill Education (India) Pvt Limited.

Haskins, G., & Thomas, M. (2018). Kindness and its many manifestations. In G. Haskins, L. Johri, & M. Thomas (Eds.), *Kindness in leadership* (pp. 8–25). Routledge.

Hays, J. M., & Kim, C. C. (2012). *Transforming leadership for the 21st century.* Xlibris Corporation.

Heifetz, R. A., Linsky, M., & Grashow, A. (2009). *The practice of adaptive leadership: Tools and tactics for changing your organization and the world.* Harvard Business Press.

Heuser, R., & Shawchuck, N. (2010). *Leading the congregation: Caring for yourself while serving others.* Abingdon Press.

Hiatt, J. (2006). *ADKAR: A model for change in business, government, and our community.* Prosci.

Hiatt, J., & Creasey, T. J. (2003). *Change management: The people side of change.* Prosci.

Holbeche, L. (2010). *HR leadership.* Routledge.

House, R. J., Dorfman, P. W., Javidan, M., Hanges, P. J., & Luque, M. F. S. (2013). *Strategic leadership across cultures: Globe study of CEO leadership behavior and effectiveness in 24 countries.* Sage.

Hromek, R., & Walsh, A. (2011). Peaceful and compassionate futures: Positive relationships as an antidote to violence. In S. Roffey (Ed.), *Positive relationships: Evidence based practice across the world* (pp. 35–54). Springer Science & Business Media.

Huiyu, G. (2018). A study on the educational strategy of using folktales in kindergarten. *Advances in Social Science, Education and Humanities Research, 264*, 757–760.

Hunt, J., & Fitzgerald, M. (2018). Introduction. In *Leadership: Regional and global perspectives* (pp. 1–21). Cambridge University Press.

Issah, M. (2018). Change leadership: The role of emotional intelligence. *SAGE Open, 8,* 1–6.

Jantz, R. C. (2017). Vision, innovation, and leadership in research libraries. *Library & Information Science Research, 39*(3), 234–241. https://doi.org/10.1016/j.lisr.2017.07.006.

Jayaraj, G. (2004). Introduction. In S. Sen, *Khasi-Jaintia folklore: Context, discourse, and history.* NFSC. www.indianfolklore.org

Johansen, B. (1992). *The new leadership literacies: Thriving in a future of extreme disruption and distributed everything.* Berrett-Koehler Publishers.

Kale, M. R. (2015). *The Hitopadesa of Narayana* (Edited with a Sanskrit Commentary "Marma-Prakasika" and Notes in English). Motilal Banarsidass Publishers Pvt. Ltd.

Kanter, R. M. (2008). *Confidence.* Random House.

Kanzunnudin, M., Rokhman, F., Sayuti, S. A., & Mardikantoro, H. B. (2018). Folklore local wisdom values of Rembang Society. *Advances in Social Science, Education and Humanities Research (ASSEHR), 247,* 340–344.

Klein, J. (2013). *The study of groups.* Taylor & Francis.

Khemka, R., & Lakkad, P. P. (2020). *Bodhkatha-Ank.* Gita Press.

Kotter, J. P. (2007). What leaders really do. In R. P. Vecchio (Ed.), *Leadership: Understanding the dynamics of power and influence in organizations* (2nd ed., pp. 23–32). University of Notre Dame Press.

Kotter, J. P. (2012). *Leading change.* Harvard Business Press.

Krahnke, K., Clinebell, S. K., & Wanasika, I. (2014). Wisdom of a leader. In J. Marques & S. Dhiman (Eds.), *Leading spiritually: Ten effective approaches to workplace spirituality* (pp. 151–166). Palgrave Macmillan.

Leider, R. J. (2008). *The power of purpose: Creating meaning in your life and work* (Easyread). ReadHowYouWant.com.

Liu, L. (2010). *Conversations on leadership: Wisdom from global management gurus.* Wiley.

Low, K. C. P. (2014). Key leadership insights and lessons from ancient wisdom. *International Journal of Business and Social Science, 5*(4), 172–180.

Luthans, F. (2010). *Organizational behaviour.* Tata McGraw-Hill Education.

Markham, D. J. (1999). *Spiritlinking leadership: Working through resistance to organizational change.* Paulist Press.

Marquardt, M. J., & Loan, P. (2006). *The manager as mentor.* Greenwood Publishing Group.

Martin, G. (2006). *Managing people and organizations in changing contexts.* Routledge.

Maxwell, J. C. (2011). *The 5 levels of leadership: Proven Steps to maximize your potential.* Center Street.

Mccall, M. W. (2010). Recasting leadership development. *Industrial and Organizational Psychology, 3*(1), 3–19.

Mehrotra, A. (2005). *Leadership styles of principals*. Mittal Publication.

Michel, A., & Gonzalez-Morales, M. G. (2013). Reactions to organizational change: An integrated model of health predictors, intervening variables, and outcomes. In A. Michel, R. Todnem, & S. Oreg (Eds.), *The psychology of organizational change viewing change from the employee's perspective* (pp. 65–92). Cambridge University Press.

Miller-Perrin, C., & Mancuso, E. K. (2014). *Faith from a positive psychology perspective*. Springer.

Mintzberg, H. (1989). *Mintzberg on management: Inside our strange world of organizations*. Simon and Schuster.

Muller, E. (2000). Personality in business. In P. Krass (Ed.), *The book of management wisdom: Classic writings by legendary managers* (pp. 41–48). Wiley.

Nonaka, I., & Takeuchi, H. (2011). The big idea: The wise leader. *Harvard Business Review*, 1–19.

Northouse, P. G. (2008). *Introduction to leadership: Concepts and practice*. Sage.

Nye, J. (2008). *The powers to lead*. Oxford University Press.

Patterson, E. (2017). Waking up to the power of reflection to unlock transformation in people, teams and organizations. In A. Alvinius (Ed.), *Contemporary leadership challenges* (pp. 3–26). BoD—Books on Demand.

Peterson, C., & Seligman, M. E. P. (2004). *Character strengths and virtues: A handbook and classification*. Oxford University Press.

Piercy, N. F., & Lane, N. (2009). *Strategic customer management: Strategizing the sales organization*. Oxford University Press.

Poddhar, H. (1950). *Upyogi Kahaniya*. Gita Press.

Podolny, F. M., Khurana, R., & Besharov, M. L. (2010). Revisiting the meaning of leadership. In N. Nohria & R. Khurana (Eds.), *Handbook of leadership theory and practice: An HBS centennial colloquium on advancing leadership* (pp. 65–106). Harvard Business Press.

Pollack, J., & Algeo, C. (2015). The contribution of project management and change management to project success. *The Business & Management Review*, 6(2), 22–30.

Porter-O'Grady, T., & Malloch, K. (2009). *Innovation leadership: Creating the landscape of healthcare*. Jones & Bartlett Learning.

Rath, T., & Conchie, B. (2009). *Strengths based leadership: Great leaders, teams, and why people follow*. Gallup Press.

Riddle, D., Hoole, E. R., & Gullette, E. C. D. (2015). Introduction. In D. Riddle, E. C. D. Gullette, & E. R. Hoole (Eds.), *The center for creative leadership handbook of coaching in organizations* (pp. xvii–xx). Wiley.

Robertson, A. W. (2000). Management's responsibility. In P. Krass (Ed.), *The book of management wisdom: Classic writings by legendary managers* (pp. 71–80). Wiley.

Sablonnière, R. D., Bourgeois, L. F., & Najih, M. (2013). Special thematic section on "societal change" dramatic social change: A social psychological perspective. *Journal of Social and Political Psychology, 1*(1), 253–272. https://doi.org/10.5964/jspp.v1i1.14

Schwartz, D. J. (2014). *The magic of thinking big.* Penguin.

Schein, E. H., & Schein, P. A. (2018). *Humble leadership: The power of relationships, openness, and trust.* Berrett-Koehler Publishers.

Sen, S. (2004). *Khasi-Jaintia folklore: Context, discourse, and history.* NFSC. www.indianfolklore.org

Senge, P. M. (2010). *The fifth discipline: The art and practice of the learning organization* (1st ed.). Random House.

Shamir, B. (2006). Introduction: From passive recipients to active co-producers: Follower's role in the leadership process. In B. Shamir, M. Uhl-Bien, M. C. Bligh, & R. Pillai (Eds.), *Follower-centered perspectives on leadership: A tribute to the memory of James R. Meindl* (pp. ix–xxxix). IAP.

Sharma, R. N., & Sharma, R (2004). *Advanced applied psychology* (Vol. 1). Atlantic Publishers & Distributors (P) Limited.

Sinatra, G. M., & Dole, J. A. (1998). Case studies in conceptual: A social psychological perspective. In B. J. Guzzetti & C. R. Hynd (Eds.), *Change perspectives on conceptual change: Multiple ways to understand knowing and learning in a complex world* (pp. 39–54). Taylor & Francis.

Sirshree. (2018). *The source—Power of happy thoughts.* Wow Publishing Pvt. Limited.

Smith, A., & Graetz, F. M. (2011). *Philosophies of organizational change.* Edward Elgar Publishing.

Smythe, E., & Norton, A. (2011). Leadership: Wisdom in action. *Indo-Pacific Journal of Phenomenology, 11*(1), 1–11.

Sole, D., & Wilson, D. G. (2002). Storytelling in organizations: The power and traps of using stories to share knowledge in organizations. *LILA, Harvard, Graduate School of Education, 9,* 1–12.

Srinivasan, V. (2006). *New age management philosophy from ancient Indian wisdom.* New Age Management Book.

Starkey, K., & Hall, C. (2012). The spirit of leadership: New direction in leadership education. In N. Nohria, S. A. Snook, & R. Khurana (Eds.), *The handbook for teaching leadership* (pp. 81–98). Sage.

Stebbins, G. (2015). Sustainable leadership through loving wisdom. *Journal of Sustainability Education, 9*(3), 1–7.

Stephan, E. G., & Pace, R. W. (2002). *Powerful leadership: How to unleash the potential in others and simplify your own life.* FT Press.

Strom, M. (2013). *Lead with wisdom: How wisdom transforms good leaders into great leaders.* Wiley.

Subramoney, R. (2020). *The LAAF way: How to let go, let flow, and laugh your way to nirvana.* Notion Press.

Suleman, M. (2008). *Advanced social psychology.* Motilal Banarsidass Publishers.

Sutton, R. (2010). *Good boss, bad boss: How to be the best and learn from the worst.* Little, Brown Book Group.

Tandon, S. (2016). Exploring well being in Indian context. *Indian Anthropologist, 46*(1), 63–78.

Taylor, C. M., Cornelius, C. J., & Colvin, K. (2014). Visionary leadership and its relationship to organizational effectiveness. *Leadership & Organization Development Journal, 35*(6), 566–583. https://doi.org/10.1108/LODJ-10-2012-0130

Tiberius, V. (2018). *Well-being as value fulfillment: How we can help each other to live well.* Oxford University Press.

Train, B., Ahmed, R., Bandawe, C., Cockcroft, K., Crafford, A., Greenop, K., Stacey, M., Tomlinson, M., Tommy, J., & Dale-Jones, B. (2007). *Fresh perspectives: Introduction to psychology.* Pearson South Africa.

Vecchio, R. P. (2007). Can leadership be taught? In R. P. Vecchio (Ed.), *Leadership: Understanding the dynamics of power and influence in organizations* (2nd ed., pp. 61–68). University of Notre Dame Press.

Wallin, D. L. (2010). Looking to the future: Change leaders for tomorrow's community colleges. In D. L. Wallin (Ed.), *Leadership in an era of change: New directions for community colleges* (pp. 5–12). Wiley.

Wibbeke, E. (2010). *Global business leadership.* Butterworth-Heinemann.

Yang, S.-Y. (2011). Wisdom displayed through leadership: Exploring leadership-related wisdom. *The Leadership Quarterly, 22*(4), 616–632.

Ziegler, J. (2010). *Republic restored—Faith, fidelity, and action.* Xlibris Corporation.

Zhu, J., Liao, Z., Yam, K. C., & Johnson, R. E. (2018). Shared leadership: A state-of-the-art review and future research agenda. *The Job Annual Review, 39*, 834–852.

Index

A
Ability, 25, 43, 45, 51, 59, 78, 79,
   81, 82, 86, 89
Acting with awareness, 45, 47
Amritasya Putra, 62
Ananda, 63–65, 71
Assertive, 49, 50
Aurelius, Marcus, 5, 9, 14
Authentic leadership, 58
Autolelic individuals, 66

B
Bhoga, 62

C
Calm, 2, 6, 8, 9, 11, 13, 19, 43, 48,
   50, 68
Change, 3, 6, 8, 16, 18, 22, 25–27,
   29, 36, 38, 43, 48, 50, 52,
   79–81, 83–88, 91–94, 98
Change management, 29, 93
Cognitive, 5, 38, 39, 42, 43, 49, 70,
   78, 80, 85, 95

Commitment, 28, 29, 51, 60, 66, 85,
   94
Conscious mind, 17, 18
COVID-19 pandemic, 2

D
Describing, 45, 46, 87, 95
Development, 5, 8, 19, 38, 41, 60,
   79–81, 85–89, 92, 94
Dichotomy of control, 8
Durant, Will, 12

E
Emotional, 4, 11, 22, 24, 26, 38, 39,
   42–44, 49–51, 65, 67, 70, 82,
   83, 88, 90, 97
Emotional intelligence, 43, 51, 83
Empathetic, 50
Employees, 28, 37–40, 49, 51, 79,
   81, 83, 88, 90, 92, 94, 97, 98
Enjoy, 46, 50, 60, 71
Enthusiasm, 5, 90, 99
Epictetus, 5, 6, 8, 10, 12, 14

Ethical actions, joy, and happiness, 16, 17

Eudaimonia, 3, 6, 8

F

Flourishment, 85, 88, 90–92, 94, 96–99

Flow, 65, 66

Frankl, Victor, 5, 13, 60

Fulfilment, 3, 79, 88, 90, 91, 93, 98, 99

G

Gill, Christopher, 6, 7

Grateful, 14, 50

Greed, 17–19, 63, 64, 67, 68, 71

Group, 37, 78, 79, 82–85, 87, 89–92, 95, 98, 99

H

Hadot, Pierre, 9, 12

Happiness, 3, 4, 6, 7, 12, 13, 18, 59–61, 63–66, 68, 71, 78–80, 82, 91, 98

Hard, Robin, 6, 13

Human flourishing, 3, 4, 58, 61, 65, 71

I

Indicators for progress towards self-transformation, 21

J

Jobs, Steve, 10, 11

K

Karma yoga, 17

Knowledge, 23, 26, 30, 78, 79, 83, 85, 86, 89, 95, 97

Krishnamurti, J., vii, 4

L

Leader, 2, 16, 19, 29, 40, 51, 58–61, 63, 65–67, 71, 79–99

Leadership, 4, 5, 8, 27, 49, 50, 52, 59, 63, 71, 78–84, 86–89, 92–99

M

Meaning in life, 58–71

Memento mori, 10

Mindfulness, 37–52, 66, 84, 89, 94, 95

Moksha, 64

Morale, 80, 82, 90–92, 98, 99

Motivation, 25, 60, 64, 67, 69, 79, 80, 85, 86, 95, 97

N

Negative visualization, 11

Nietzsche, Friedrich, 10, 60

Nishkam karma, 67

Nonjudging, 45, 47

Nonreactivity, 45, 48

O

Observing, 45, 88

Obstacles in the path of self-transformation, 19

Organization, 2, 16, 17, 21, 22, 25, 27–29, 31, 32, 36–38, 40, 41, 44, 49, 51, 52, 58, 59, 66, 78, 80–82, 85, 87, 88, 90, 92, 94, 98

Organizational benefits, 40, 89

Organizational culture, 26, 28

Organizational transformation, 27–32

P
Pay attention, 41
Peace of mind, 63–65
Perception, 23, 38, 40, 61, 85
Personal benefits, 42
Phenomenology, 58, 61
Phenomenology study, 58, 61
Physical, 4, 23, 24, 26, 42, 49, 51, 52, 60, 61, 67, 69, 70
Plato, 3, 10
Pleonexia, 67
Positive, 18, 22, 44, 48, 51, 52, 58, 61, 66, 71, 78, 85–87, 89, 90, 93–95, 98
Presence of meaning, 59
Process of change, 18, 25, 84

R
Resistance to change, 22, 24, 25, 28

S
Search for meaning, 59
Self-realization, 20, 30, 64, 71, 79
Self-transformation, 16–21, 25, 26, 28, 30–32, 80, 98
Seneca, 5, 9, 11, 12, 14
Sensitive, 50, 94
Serenity Prayer, 7
Servant leaders, 58, 67
Seven energies that drive your personality, 26
Skills, 26, 66, 86, 88, 90, 93–95, 99
Socrates, 3, 6
Spiritual, 2–4, 17–19, 22, 24, 26, 29, 36, 42, 44, 58–61, 63, 70, 71, 80, 89, 95
Stockdale, James, 5, 8

Stoicism, 2, 5–9, 13
Stories, 60, 81, 85, 86, 93, 95
Strategy, 6, 26, 80, 81, 83, 85, 88, 89, 96, 98
Stress, 5, 6, 8, 17, 30, 37, 39, 40, 42, 48, 49, 51, 52, 58, 60, 61, 68
Subconscious mind, 17, 18, 20, 92
Super conscious mind, 17, 18, 20

T
The Palgrave Handbook of Workplace Well-Being, 5
Transformational leadership, 61, 82

V
Values, 2, 6, 18, 24–26, 28, 31, 41, 48, 58, 59, 61, 63–65, 68, 69, 78, 79, 81–83, 86, 88, 89, 95, 97
Vasanas, 69
Viragya, 68
Vision, 17, 27, 79, 82, 85–88, 96
Viveka, 68

W
Well-being, 3, 4, 8, 25, 37, 40, 44, 51, 59–61, 64, 66–71, 78–80, 82, 85, 88, 90, 91, 94, 96, 98
Wisdom, 2–4, 6, 7, 19, 62, 68, 78, 80–89, 91, 94, 96–99
Workplace, 3, 5, 58, 60, 79, 85, 87, 91, 94
Workplace wellbeing, 3, 85, 91, 93, 97, 98
Worldly passions, 61, 64, 67, 68, 71